Praise for
MIND SKIL

"Navigating the brave new world of business requires a radically new set of skills. In "Mind Skills," Linda Bjork and Stephanie Mitchko offer not just a roadmap for acquiring those skills but also practical, pragmatic advice on applying them to any challenge or opportunity we face."

~Adam C. Hall, Author of Divine Genius and
CEO at the Genius Studio, Inc.

"Mind Skills is both a practical reflection on developing a successful business culture and an insightful exploration of our own humanity. This long-overdue book is filled with useful information."

~Chief Dwaine Perry, Elected Chief of the
Ramapo Munsee Lunaape Indian Nation

"Linda Bjork and Stephanie Mitchko challenge conventional truths and lay out a new roadmap to success and leaving a legacy. "Mind Skills" shows you how to bring more of your unique brilliance and talent to the table, and how to nurture and develop current and next generation talent. If idea-generation, innovation, and knowing what's next are missing ingredients from your life (or your teams), make sure to read this book."

~Pär Roosvall, CEO & Chairman, NFT Group

"Fantastic!! Mind Skills is a tremendously authentic and empowering summary of critical focus areas for playing in the Big Leagues in both business and life. A spectacular read! I particularly loved the framing of Toxic People and Toxic Behavior. So true!"

~John Schanz, former Chief Network Officer, Comcast Cable

"The quality of your thinking determines the quality of your life. If you agree, you will want to read Mind Skills. Linda and Stephanie's new book offers a vigorous work-out for your mind, body, and soul. I recommend it wholeheartedly."

~Robert Holden, author of Shift Happens! and Higher Purpose

"The unabashed honesty gained from their own experiences and hard-won wisdom navigating the rocky and revealing road to success gives this enormously insightful and empowering book its authenticity and insights to support readers on their own journeys to unleash their potential. Rather than being role models to follow, Linda and Stephanie show how to become embodied soul models; as heart-centered and servant-leaders to most effectively empower the flow of the future and, vitally, for the good of the whole."

~Dr Jude Currivan, cosmologist, conscious business leader, author and co-founder WholeWorld-View

"Leading with the bywords Grace and Heart, the authors of Mind Skills openly and honestly share real-life stories and the abiding skills that will guide readers through career and life challenges."

~Jennifer Yohe, Chief Procurement Officer, Altice USA

In an age where leaders face extraordinary challenges alongside unprecedented opportunities, this wonderful book by Linda Bjork and Stephanie Mitchko offers sage insights into the infinite pathways and limitless treasures of one's own mind. Filled with illuminating and entertaining personal stories of growth, the authors take us on a journey through loss, failure, resilience and ultimately towards sustained success and excellence. Most importantly, they lay out a game plan where anyone who is in a leadership role, or aspires to be, can meet the challenges of the modern world to become masters of our own destiny with no ceiling on what we and our teams can achieve. I commend Linda and Stephanie on this most practical and powerful contribution to the field of leadership development.

~Ben Bowler, Executive Director, Unity Earth

MIND SKILLS
Unleash Your Potential to Lead in the Big Leagues

by Linda Bjork and Stephanie Mitchko

The Inner Business Institute and Rare Air Leadership

Cover photo by: Becky Yee, Color Wheel Studios, NYC

The fonts and graphics in this book are licensed with Adobe Creative Suite, Adobe Stock images, and iStock.

ISBN: 979-8-9884103-0-0 (sc)

ISBN: 979-8-9884103-1-7 (hc)

ISBN: 979-8-9884103-2-4 (e)

Library of Congress Control Number: 2023909880

Bjork/Mitchko date: 09/15/2023

Mind Skills

Dedications:

From Linda to
Harley, Lion King, and Lucyboy

From Stephanie to
Natasha, Nicholai, and Alex

Table of Contents

Introduction

Welcome to the Big Leagues. What are the big leagues, anyway? Is it receiving an Emmy® Award? A half-billion-dollar business budget? Being dressed by fashion gurus? Are they defined by private air travel, a team of personal assistants, or having thousands of employees below your name on the org chart? Receiving recognition and admiration are thought of as being in the big leagues.

We've lived it and can tell you that it's really none of those. Those things are just perks.

The real big leagues, a place of impact that matters, are inside you.

You'll know you're in the big leagues when you can hold space for life's paradoxes and complexities; when you feel liberated from the burden of other people's judgments and can instead focus on what really matters to you; when you remain kind in the face of criticism, care deeply about your team's wellbeing, and let people be their unique selves while helping them to feel engaged and empowered.

The big leagues have little or nothing to do with the size of your company or the loftiness of your title. It doesn't even have to do with fame or followers. Being in the big leagues means being aligned and clear-minded so you can influence meaningful change, wherever you are. You know you have made it when your mind skills and presence can alchemize people and situations to grow to their fullest potential.

The big leagues start within yourself. Because you are a big deal. Let's bring it out in the world.

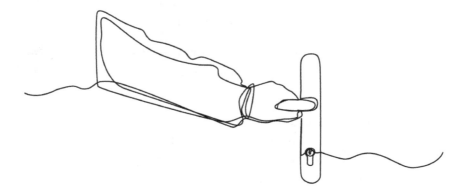

One
Exit with Grace

Yes, exits. It might seem backward, and you may be wondering why a book about achieving leadership success is opening with a discussion of Exits. Shouldn't we begin with advice on how to reach the level of success that will afford you a fabulous exit?

In a word, no. One of our key observations about success in the big leagues is that the handling of exits matters tremendously, whether it's your own departure or someone else's.

- Leaders who create strong cultures and great opportunities don't see a constant churn of talent exiting.

- Professionals who know *when* and *how* to exit their roles make better career moves than those who don't.

- Knowing how to exit relationships that no longer serve you is an advantage.

Exits are one of the biggest headaches for business leaders. It's discouraging to watch talent choose to leave. Replacing them is difficult and expensive. Separations are often painful on a personal level, too, even if the relationship wasn't great. Even when you *do* want someone to exit, it can have a demoralizing effect on the remaining team members.

You'll be touched by every type of exit as you navigate the big leagues. Knowing how to create healthy exits at any scale or level is a key mind skill.

In our experience and understanding, the type of mind that best supports healthy exits has a quality of *grace*. From a mind skills perspective, grace is an internal state of goodwill. Grace allows us to honor people and events. It lets us maintain a sense of calm strength in the face of difficulty.

The challenge of living in a state of grace is that it's hard to do. We all have automated mind functions that can lead us to react to exits with the polar opposite of grace. Separations can make us feel abandoned, betrayed, or irrelevant and lead us to become stressed, defensive, or even aggressive.

In this chapter, we'll take you through our most important findings on the mental and emotional aspects of exits (no matter which side of the table you're on) and offer practical advice for navigating the exit mechanism.

Stephanie: *"People were stunned to learn that I was leaving a C-suite role at a Fortune 100 company, AKA "the top of the mountain." Why would anyone willingly exit a top job? Well, I've had many exits over the course of my career. Most were occasioned by better offers that would bring new challenges and more opportunities to further ascend the peaks of success.*

Admittedly, things are different at the top of a high mountain than they are at lower levels (or from atop a smaller mountain). Your view is better, clearer. Executive support is stellar. Your actions have greater impact. But the air is thinner, while you still must perform at an enhanced level. Lateral opportunities are fewer. The stakes are much higher. You're under greater scrutiny. If you're not in sync with your colleagues and peers, your days will be overly strenuous and maybe even dangerous to your career, reputation, and health.

But the real difference at the top is that you now are in the lion's den.

Don't become distracted by the lofty view and forget that you are in a culture of lions: The company's top leadership. It can be easy to slide into an "everything is fine" mindset, because, come on, it's pretty darn comfortable at the top... until it's not.

After a few years of sitting comfortably in a C-suite, I began to suspect there was a mismatch. It began as a sneaky feeling that was tied to small disappointments. Nothing big. Nothing dramatic. Just my observations of shifts in the styles and nuances of those around me. Always pay attention to your intuition! It may be telling you that it's time to leave.

Deciding to leave and being asked to leave are really the same thing. It happens when a mismatch can't be resolved. Whether it's because of a bad overall fit, or a situation that wasn't addressed, whatever is stirring in you will manifest in one of two ways. Either you'll initiate your own exit, or eventually be escorted to the door.

In the big leagues, a telltale sign of a mismatch is when you start to feel out of the loop. Information isn't flowing, and you find yourself chasing it. On a great executive team, information is shared, and objectives are made clear to all. When there's radio silence, you really need to pay attention.

Another revealing sign is changes in communication styles. Your boss might be the type who prefers to review presentations and provide feedback before you deliver it at a meeting. Take note if it suddenly changes. If the boss no longer wants to confer on meeting content or strategy, it's a strong signal that changes are coming.

Think about it from your own perspective as a leader and assess your own boss the same way. Your job is to make sure your team members remain engaged. If you stopped paying attention to a team member's input, it's probably because you have something else in mind for them. Might be a role change, a re-org, or an exit. Your lack of engagement signals to that person that something is wrong. This is true at any level of an organization.

The drawback of being at the top in business is that there's not much room for reshuffling. Space is limited and egos are huge. You must be laser-focused on honing your talents and developing your mind skills as you work to make it in the big leagues. Every role eventually comes to its natural conclusion, so don't get too comfortable.

I realized in my own process that a feeling of continual misalignment in any facet of life is a red flag that we must not ignore. As our conscious-ness grows we see things we couldn't see before, even other, higher mountains that may better align with our goals. That's when we know it's time to go.

In my case, as I was leaving, I realized that I was leaving behind an old part of me and moving on to a new journey. Something a wise young mountain climber once told me still resonates:

"Reaching the summit is not the time to celebrate. Half the trip is still ahead of you." ~ Alex Mitchko

As I prepared for my own descent, I made up my mind that this time I would be very present in the process, and I made a point of examining my inner dialogues all along the way. See, the perks that await on the mountaintop are fantastic. The big stages, far-reaching platform, high-level conversations, fun offsites, and constant VIP treatment. Walking away from that necessitates a bit of ego-wrestling, and self-reflection can be surprisingly painful. It wasn't from the thought of leaving the rarefied air. I've lived long enough to stop defining myself by outside value markers. No, the pain I felt was connected to my teams, people whom I had grown to love and respect along our shared journey. People who looked to me for leadership guidance and clarity, who had felt seen and heard by me and had helped me grow as well. That was the part that hurt to leave behind. Almost every executive I know says they miss their teams more than they miss the trappings of a senior role.

What I've gained on this descent is a deepening of grace. Navigating previous departures, I thought of "grace" as leaving on good terms, continuing to nurture existing relationships, and not throwing anything hard at anyone as I sailed out the door. But this last fall from on high has enriched my journey of grace. With intention, I examined my ego bruises and heartache to sort out what hurt and why. Initially, feelings of fear, anger, relief, happiness, and sadness swirled inside me, but when they subsided, I found that I could trust myself in a new way. I felt connected to a sea of wonderful people and energies beyond the specificity of a certain role or organization.

We will explore the actual mind skills needed to make graceful exits in any area of life. Being prepared inside and out is key, not just in a contractual sense but also in having a clear plan for your life and career. Know what your exit looks like before you even start your role. Make a conscious decision to treat all exits with reverence so that when your time comes you can leave with the respect of everyone around you.

When it's your own exit, it can be hard to acknowledge that your presence is not needed or wanted, that you are replaceable, that the company will move on without you. Dismissals can sting—or be very freeing. Choose the latter. It's easy—and sometimes tempting—to look back and blame others, but it won't change anything. Respect yourself and honor both the past and the future. Make your final words an authentic "How can I help?" and then go.

Choosing to feel liberated is a type of grace I am grateful to experience every day. I've upgraded my compass and am eager to see where it takes me. Readers who know me may be wondering if I've had some kind of spiritual stroke. Don't worry. I'm still a razor-sharp tech enthusiast, just one with a wide streak of healthy skepticism and not annoyingly happy every day like Linda is. Or as she translates it from Swedish, 'a happy little shit.'"

Linda: "As an executive coach, I listen to and support professionals who are mired in conflicts and uncertainty but want to get to the next level and do great, fulfilling work. The subject of exits—preparing for them, enduring them, and recovering from toxic ones—comes up often. Exits are such a triggering event that people can fail to see the situation's tremendous potential.

Exits must be part of your awareness before you enter any situation, *whether it's a relationship, a role, an investment, or a partnership.*

One of my clients—let's call him Sam—is a prime example of why it's important to have an exit plan right from the beginning. Before he was summoned to the big leagues, Sam worked at a smaller firm. Friends, family, and even co-workers told him he was meant for bigger things, and he suspected as much himself. When a large company courted him for a C-suite position, he was ready to jump.

In his haste to seize the exciting new opportunity, though, Sam failed to think about his eventual exit and consider the possible human and relational circumstances that might trigger him to instigate it himself. But the human brain has an uncanny ability to create a vague mental picture and fill in the missing information with unfounded assumptions and manufactured details, and Sam just assumed that things would work out. He never imagined that others in the C-suite might not be aligned with the company vision or would be unwilling to support efforts to move the company forward. It seemed so basic to him that he simply didn't check into the "soft parts" before he accepted the role: Values alignment. Collaborative approaches. The degree to which self-promoting executives would undermine day-to-day operations.

The events of his very first meeting with his new C-suite team would force him out just a few years later.

On Sam's first day, he was chauffeured to a swanky offsite meeting and introduced as a key addition to the leadership team. Everyone seemed happy to have him there, except for one person—who turned out to be his "surprise" boss. Another C-suite member had squeezed himself into the org chart to have Sam report to him. In his own team meeting later that day the new boss said, "I'm not really sure why Sam is here, or why he has his title, but apparently the CEO thought this was a good idea, so we'll figure it out."

All Sam's ideas, projects, team input or work output would be questioned in the same way. "I don't know if having you here is a good idea" echoed in the feedback Sam received, from his first day to his last.

Had Sam been intentional when exiting his "small pond" position, taken the time to gain clarity around the reporting structure, had a few vibe meetings with the new boss and CEO and his own direct reports, he could have avoided some of the most painful and demoralizing years of his career.

I remind my clients to check in often with the "soft parts." They pack the hardest punch."

Mind Skills

Welcome to the Mind Skills section of this chapter! We presume you are a competent professional with business experience and a reputation you want to preserve. Being human is hard in general, but it's especially painful related to exits. We get it. Let's skip ahead and look at what goes on inside us when we're up against that exit door.

Exits trigger complex thoughts and emotions in us, whether we're atop the mountain or just achieving the first summit. Our responses are fast and automatic. Words like *end, termination,* and *separation* spark feelings of abandonment, rejection, and diminishment. Feelings of fear and helplessness can bring on freakouts or shutdowns. It's grace that will get you through this.

From a mind skills standpoint, there are two major obstacles along our road to grace:

1. Our nervous systems dictate our choices (see below for *Million-Dollar Questions*)

2. Humans prefer not to take responsibility for ourselves, thank you very much (read on for *Wherever We Go*)

Million-Dollar Questions

"Should I stay, or should I go?" might be the most important question people ever ask themselves, personally or professionally. As leaders, we also have to grapple with *"Should I invest in this person, or is it time to push them out?"* To make better choices about such big questions, let's look at the part of us

that dictates many of our reactions: The human nervous system.

Start from this basis: We are hardwired to prefer what's familiar to us, even when the situation or possible outcomes aren't great. Our central nervous systems perceive familiarity as safety, because if we recognize something it means we've already encountered and survived it. Familiarity will always have an outsized influence on our decision-making because our nervous systems keep making decisions based on our subconscious programming—which is, by the way, largely in place by the time we're seven years old.

Whatever your nervous system perceives as "familiar" is likely to win. Not necessarily because it's best for you but because your nervous system is still calling the shots. That's why we all keep doing things that don't work.

However! There is a glaring exception to the familiarity rule, and it's this: Our brains do not *want* us to take an honest and open look at our own garbage. It would be uncomfortable, maybe even painful, so our automated response tells us not to do it. So instead of taking responsibility and working through the hard things, we run off to the next place, even though the current place might have been fine after some communication and tweaks. This is why employers scrutinize employment dates on résumés. If there have been numerous exits, it's important to learn whether the moves were healthy and circumstantial, or if the candidate lacks the courage to manage discomfort and push through hard times.

Leaders who want to make good decisions have to start with understanding our nervous systems. Its prime directive is to keep our bodies alive and safe. But its concept of "safe" often has little to do with the situation that's in front of us. Each of us operates on a great big database of our life experiences that has been programmed into us since we were kids. It remembers everything that has happened to us. It also remembers how we responded.

Here's a classic example. You stay in an undesirable (or untenable) situation because the idea of leaving feels unsafe. Even if you're telling yourself you want to leave, your own nervous system is not okay with an unknown future because it remembers times your moves didn't work out. At least you know the territory, says the little voice inside you. You can handle the negatives, and now that you think about it, the benefits package is great, and another place probably won't cover dental. Case closed. You stay.

But then you feel trapped and resentful and unhealthy behaviors take over. You behave in ways you're not proud of. Complain to anyone who'll listen. Blame people and situations. Making risky or rash decisions. Then, just when you think you couldn't feel any worse, you get fired. And now you're leaving behind colleagues who aren't very impressed with your performance or behavior and who probably won't offer glowing endorsements. This wrench went into your career wheel when your nervous system made choices that weren't in your best interest.

You might be on the other side of the table and dealing with a toxic team member who is also your highest performer. They produce stellar numbers but ruin morale. You're aware that this one toxic person is making the rest of the team miserable, but you don't act. Why? Familiarity again, and probably twofold:

1.   You evaluate performance based only on familiar KPI metrics and don't consider a person's impact on the team and others.

2.   You are uncomfortable having hard and honest conversations. If you weren't you'd coach the toxic person.

Mind skills will help you avoid these mistakes and limit unwanted exits from your team. People should be given a fair chance, but when they might cause real harm, it's time for them to go. When our nervous systems are making our decisions, we can lose touch with this basic leadership principle. Let's lay a solid foundation for the mind skills to come, by first learning to regulate our fear responses.

A small but great way to start is by finding a stress-reduction practice that works for you. Mindfulness-based stress reduction, Heart-Brain Coherence, or a guided meditation with a soothing soundtrack may help your nervous system to regulate itself and find the sweet spot between calm and alertness. A regular stress-reduction practice strengthens the parasympathetic nervous system, that regulates our fear responses, stress, upset, anger, anxiety, depression, apathy, and grief. When this system is strong, grace is an easy choice—even in the face of exits.

A stress-reduction or meditation practice is critical for leaders (and great for team members too). It's basic mental hygiene.

Wherever We Go...

Jon Kabat Zinn, creator of Mindfulness Based Stress Reduction (MBSR), titled one of his books with a quote from his own father: "*Wherever you go, there you are.*"

When we contemplate a personal or professional exit, we might think leaving will solve all our problems. But we would be wrong because wherever you go next, there you'll be. Same nervous system, same subconscious, same vibe, drawing in the same old situations. We are not suggesting that you shouldn't leave a situation that isn't good for you, but life tends to reflect back who we are, so we recommend you first make a good honest go at understanding and healing yourself. As much as hurt people *hurt* people, healed people *heal* people. Leading meaningful change in the big leagues requires a healed, whole person who has shed old and limiting ways and is prepared to orchestrate big changes, collaborative efforts, and groundbreaking innovation.

When we reflect on deeper questions about who we are and what we choose to admit into our lives, we are bound to find old, unhelpful programming in our minds. That's what we want to work on. *Why do I tolerate poor treatment? What's my role in teaching people how to treat me? Why is this little voice telling me I don't deserve better? Why do I believe it?*

We might discover that we contribute to difficult relationships. Maybe what's not working at work has less to do with the bosses, co-workers, traffic, stupid project tool, creaky desk chair, or other annoying external factor. If we're honest and vulnerable we may find that what's not working for us may very well be... us. That's not to say that we are to blame for everything, but we do have to recognize and acknowledge responsibility for the part played by our own programming.

Both of us have spent a lot of time in the hiring seat. We've had candidates walk us through their résumé and assure us that all five of their exits in the past seven years were due to bad bosses or poor team cohesion. Everyone has been so mean to them!

Top thought leaders in cellular biology and consciousness believe our lives are basically a printout of our subconscious minds, so we learn to ask ourselves: *What are the recurring patterns in these negative experiences? What conflict or unpleasantness keeps showing up in my life? What themes come up both at work and at home?* Mature analysis leads to breakthroughs.

We've made ourselves look at some pretty ugly recurring patterns in our own lives. For both of us, the overarching theme is *ego*, with its competitiveness, its determination to shine, its need to always be right. And where better for it than the workplace? Business is built on the achieving, striving ego!

Identifying whether ego is wrong or bad is not as important as recognizing when it's *dangerous*. The ego is a perceived survival mechanism. But its instinct for self-preservation will stop at nothing. It will do everything it can to take over.

Many in business allow ego to wrest away their authentic power in exchange for raises, promotions, wins, more raises, more promotions. Until suddenly all the competing and posturing doesn't feel satisfying anymore. Things that were important to you have lost their appeal.

When you reflect on past exits, don't be surprised to discover that much of the pain of leaving a role, a company, or a relationship comes from leaving that old part of you behind. The person you were when you signed up for that role is probably not who you are anymore. What you wanted from a relationship has evolved since you entered it. Acknowledge that you are leaving the old you behind. It takes courage to admit that you were a person you don't want to be anymore. But honor the old you before you let them go. Take a moment to mourn if it will make you feel better. As you assess what you are leaving behind and decide who you are ready to become, you move forward and heal yourself.

Like a snake that sheds its skin, you leave the old you behind and exit the situation that doesn't serve the upgraded, healed you.

Your life may be presenting all kinds of exits—jobs, partnerships, relationships, companies, industries—but letting go of someone you no longer want to be is the best exit.

The Grace Factor

If we view an exit only as an ending, we might miss the new opportunities that lay beyond. A rejection can be viewed as a redirection, a transition to something new. Endings and beginnings form the basis of our careers and relationships. The math is obvious: Bad exits have a negative impact; graceful exits add value.

Grace has many connotations, so let's outline it as it relates to the exiting process. This will be one of this book's very few acronym gambits, we promise.

G - Get clear on what's right for you

R - Recondition your fear triggers

A - Anticipate good things

C - Connect with gratitude, support, and possibilities

E - Exit on your terms—with your inner smile intact!

Get clear on what's right for you

If you're not clear on what's right for you, you'll make choices based on external pressures. Usually these take the form of other people's needs and priorities, and your best interest isn't their top priority. Which is fine! That's *your* job! And no one knows more than you do about what's in your heart.

Most successful leaders are at least a little bit eccentric. They don't feel compelled to be like everyone else. Neither should you. What's right for you may never have existed before! Our best contributions to the world are the ones that use our own unique combination of talents. We know we're on the right track when we feel a sense of excitement and even joy. When you're clear on what's right for you, what *feels* right for you, decisions around exits become a lot easier.

Recondition your fear triggers

If you don't recondition your fear triggers, you'll always be controlled by your ego's reactions, rather than reaping the rewards of proactive behavior. Whatever your age, your reactions are dictated by things you saw and experienced early in life. Our subconscious mind—our nervous system's database—runs on old information until you heal and upgrade it.

We see executives and managers being manipulated and making unforced errors when their fear triggers are set off. Many people with narcissistic or sociopathic tendencies go far in business. They're around and they are expert at sniffing out triggers. If you recondition your fear triggers, you will make calm, informed, and rational decisions that allow you to go further than you may have dared to imagine.

Anticipate good things

If you don't anticipate good things, you are using your neurology against yourself. Our brains have what's called "mirror neurons." They react to our own thoughts and actions in the same way they would if we observed those same thoughts or actions from others. If you expect the worst of people and situations, don't be surprised when they deliver.

Some people walk into a meeting or interview anticipating negative feedback, anxious that they'll say the wrong thing or seem incompetent. That defensive and insecure vibe can be sensed from down the hall and only increases the likelihood of your fears coming to pass. If you expect the worst from a situation you will fold like cheap lawn furniture under the burden of your own anxiety.

Instead, change your approach. Anticipate good things. Meetings are learning opportunities! You can always find a safe place inside yourself from which you can observe and learn. When you share what you find interesting, and focus on learning from dialogue and feedback, it's impossible to be seen as incompetent.

Connect with gratitude, support and possibilities

Gratitude is a primary doorway to many of the sometimes-intangible conditions that beget business success. Operate from a sincere sense of gratitude and you'll find support in other people too. You belong to an interconnected and social humanity, with endless possibilities before you. If you disconnect from the energy of that flow, you are disconnected from everything.

Gratitude operates inside us by teaching our brains what to recognize and value to create more gratitude, and also in the relational space between ourselves and others, all of us longing to be appreciated. Don't underestimate the power of saying "thank you" or just checking in. Those who exit with the most and best opportunities before them are those who have fostered an "attitude of gratitude" and stayed connected to industry friends, colleagues, and others they've met along the way.

Exit on your terms - with your inner smile intact!

As you get further in your inner work, you'll become in touch with your own talent, joy, and fulfillment—your inner smile. Your goals will become more internal and less external. You'll sense where you should or shouldn't go, and what's for you or not for you. Exits will be clearly marked. And if your boss beats you to it and lets you go, you won't be offended. It was time anyway. While leaving is usually more fun than being dismissed, the result is the same. Use your focus to remove the noise. Then accept what is there.

Knowing ourselves on a deeper level brings joy and energy to life and helps you learn why you're here. Our hope is that you'll become awake and aware enough to choose your own exits and new beginnings in every area of your life and find joy along the way.

A beautiful aspect of a high grace factor is that it resolves one of humanity's biggest fears: That of the unknown. Grace is a big and elegant sensation. It reminds us that there is a bigger picture, a vast connectedness, a place where greatness is born. If we tune into it, we can feel the grace that is a source of peace, presence, and even awe. What a beautiful way to enter your next chapter.

--

"You cannot stay on the summit forever; you have to come down again. So why bother in the first place? Just this: What is above knows what is below, but what is below does not know what is above. One climbs, one sees. One descends, one sees no longer, but one has seen. There is an art of conducting oneself in the lower regions by the memory of what one saw higher up. When one can no longer see, one can at least still know."

~ Rene Daumal

--

Two
Owning Your Shit

Mind shifts about taking responsibility for our messes usually announce themselves with a rude awakening rather than a gentle tap. We wish we could say that we'd always owned our own shit and sailed smoothly from thoughtful insights to mature decisions. But no. Mind shifts around taking responsibility tend to be incited by a messy event dropping on top of other stressors and forcing us to find another way.

Stephanie: *"My triggering event was my divorce. I had three young children and was a senior executive in a very demanding role. Divorce isn't something anyone hopes or plans for. Even when it's amicable, the process is emotionally taxing for everyone involved. It just sucks.*

If you had asked me at the time, I would have said I was still showing up at work in top form. I was using my hard-won superpowers to make things go the way I wanted. My capacity for logic was intact and my intellect was undeniable, but the results told a different story. Why

17

didn't people see things the way I did? Why was I always being misun-derstood? Why weren't my projects flowing as they used to? Why did everything seem so difficult?

Things were spiraling out of control, and I had exhausted every option from my then-limited toolbox when the breaking point arrived. I had to do the thing I hated the most: I had to ask for help.

Trusted friends and colleagues suggested I talk to a counselor or ther-apist. As an executive, I was used to receiving coaching and mentoring, so it made sense. I may not be comfortable asking for help, but I am open to trying new things.

Admittedly, I was not a fan of psychology. Rambling on to a stranger about my personal life didn't feel like a good use of my time. And what do they know anyway? I mean, really! I am an engineer! If I can't figure it out, how can they?

A friend referred me to her own longtime therapist, "Sue." I was sure Sue wouldn't be able to help me, but it felt like this was my only remain-ing option. When I learned that her office was only a short drive from my office, my last excuse was gone. I arranged an appointment, still feeling resistant.

The day was sunny and the drive was easy, giving me plenty of time to think about what a waste of time this was.

Sue met me at her office door with a warm smile. The space was neat and homey, with a couch along one wall (of course!) opposite a comfortable-looking chair. A small corner desk held a tea set and an electric kettle.

Sue motioned me toward the couch and settled into the facing chair. Once seated, I introduced myself.

"Nice to meet you, Stephanie," she said. "So, tell me what's been going on."

Right to the point. No small talk. I liked that. I rattled off a litany of the things that were happening to me.

"I'm going through a divorce. My husband is being an ass. The family court system is a mess. People who don't know us and don't actually give a shit get to make decisions for my family. My job is incredibly stressful, and I haven't been promoted in years, while my peers—mostly men—have moved up." I went on longer, but you get the gist.

Sue offered me a cup of tea and I couldn't think of a reason to refuse, so she went to the desk and prepared two cups. When we were comfortably settled with our steaming cups, Sue looked me straight in the eye and asked, "So what is your part in all that?"

I was stunned. I didn't say anything aloud, but I was thinking "What the hell? And fuck you!"

Sue introduced me to the concept of Owning My Shit. My work had begun.

It's been a long journey, but one with infinite benefits. I learned that acknowledging and owning my own messes would transform my life. In other words, becoming mindful, conscious, and aware of your own part in situations is the first step to changing them."

Mind Skills

Personal responsibility is a fascinating concept. Understanding that we are responsible for our own lives usually is a two-step process:

1. Being incredibly offended by the suggestion that I had anything to do with any of this *waves arms*

2. Being incredibly empowered after acknowledging that I had something to do with what is going on in my life! The possibilities open right up.

Many people get offended at the idea that we created our life situations (all or part) ourselves, because it feels like criticism. *You're saying that I made this mess because I suck, or because I hate myself.* But your life is not proof of your ability or smarts. It's a manifestation of what's going on in your subconscious mind, and what's in your subconscious is not your fault. (More to come on that.)

Learning to own our own messes comes with an understanding that things happen long before they actually happen, and that your attitude has tremendous influence on outcomes.

Just as it takes a lot of ideas, planning, resources, and time to build a building, it takes a lot of thought, feeling, action, and energy to create a personal reality.

An important tool in Mindfulness Intelligence is *How Life Happens*, a three-step process of managing our attitude toward life so we can make better choices and attract better opportunities. You'll probably have seen significant results by the time you get through Step 2. Regular internal check-ins and course corrections will take you the rest of the way.

How Life Happens

Step 1: Life Happens <u>To</u> Me

An attitude of "Life happens *to* me" puts us in the back seat instead of the driver's seat. If we're not behind the wheel, other people and external events are in control. When we hand over the car keys, we surrender our autonomy, integrity, and purpose. It feels like nothing good is available to us.

Not that there aren't upsides to this! For example:

- **One:** We get to blame other people when the traffic is heavy or we miss the exit or arrive at the wrong place. *It's not my fault! I wasn't even driving!*

- **Two:** We can complain about anything and anyone! In fact, some of our relationships are based on complaining. We connect by bitching about the boss. We bond over our terrible exes. We unite in our resentment of people who are naturally thin. Yay! Now we have new friends.

- **Three:** Other people will take care of us! When everything is disappointing and nothing is our fault, someone will feel sorry for us and come to our rescue. They take out the trash, pick up the check, and give us attention and hugs. Purr.

This makes some people not even want to try to wrest back their car key. Eventually we don't even trust ourselves to drive. We become accustomed to a life that's based on other people's plans, dreams, and expectations—until something feels off and we realize we've been asking the same questions over and over and gotten no satisfying answers. *Why am I not where I thought I'd be by now? Why are people so mean? Why is life so unfair? Why does this keep happening to me?*

At this stage we might believe that the universe just doesn't want us to live well. Our innate confirmation bias means that when we look for bad energy, we find it. When other people drive the car of Our Life poorly, or along the wrong route, resentment builds up in our minds and bodies and we become less forgiving, less generous, less kind. Without a mindful approach, we can end up in that back seat forever.

There's another option, though. Your situation need not dictate your attitude, but your attitude often dictates your life situation. Outcomes start in the mind. You make the choices.

Step 2: Life Happens <u>For</u> Me

Oh, the remarkable power of a tiny preposition. When we presume that "Life happens *for* me," a whole new level of ease becomes accessible to us. You don't have to wait for a secret signal to appear in the sky. You can make a new choice right now about how to approach life.

Maybe things are happening *for* you. Even the bad things. Think about it. A rejection isn't automatically a tragedy. Often it can be a protection or a redirection. Have you ever had something you initially considered a disaster turn out to be a blessing? Maybe you missed out on a job opportunity, but it meant you were available when your dream role opened up. You might have missed your train but made a new dear friend while waiting for the next one. Or you didn't get the funding you sought, but it gave you time to improve your business plan.

21

We don't always know what's best for us. And sometimes perfectly-executed plans don't bring the expected results. When you believe life happens *for* you, you won't waste time, money, and energy sulking about missed chances, attacking people who should pay for your misfortune, or crying behind a closed door. Instead, two big things will happen: You'll be awake for the lessons offered, and you'll be conscious enough to recognize better opportunities.

A small change in attitude can create a seismic shift. The simple concept that you are responsible for your life puts you in the driver's seat. Caveat: You will have to put on your grownup pants and maybe even eat some crow. You will have to say things like *I made a mistake. I took a wrong turn. I am sorry. I messed up. I will right this wrong. I take full responsibility.*

This change helped Stephanie to recalibrate her life situation in the wake of her divorce. No more blaming others. It didn't mean she hadn't been wronged, or that storms hadn't blown in and messed things up. She just shifted to owning her role in it instead of reacting to other people's behavior.

It's incredible how new opportunities appear when we believe life happens *for* us and are always willing to explore how we brought on the situation with our own choices. It's liberating to inventory our own participation, identify the patterns of the thoughts, feelings and actions that led us there, and take responsibility for the energy we bring to situations. When we trust ourselves to make mature assessments and stay alert to opportunities, we start trusting life more too. Life wants us to be well.

Flip the switch today. Decide that life happens *for* you and get the support you need to stay a course of integrity, responsibility, and purpose. Drive your own life.

Step 3: Life Happens <u>Through</u> Me

When you feel ready, an additional level of attitude is here for your consideration. We have traveled from Step 1 (disempowerment; taking no personal responsibility) to Step 2 (empowered; taking personal responsibility). In Step 3 we put aside our ego and become a co-creator of life.

When we allow life to happen *through* us, it becomes apparent that life itself also wants to make things happen, and that we can be vessels for that evolutionary essence. An inner voice whispers that it's time to start or build or create something—a bridge between points A and B, a new way of educating children, or a digital platform that will change the world—and we feel a pull, a life-affirming excitement. Life happens *through* us because change and growth happen *through* us.

Don't be surprised when two people have the same innovative idea at the same time. It's just two individuals responding to the same evolutionary prompt. Ideas that arise from universal inspiration can receive support through universal intervention. What they do with it and how well they execute depends largely on adherence to Step 3. "Life happens through us" doesn't mean we're in charge. It will often be quite evident we're not. But when we see clearly that people and situations are interconnected and interdependent, and competition and comparison are futile, we can trust that resources will appear when the timing is right. We don't have to live amid stress or worries. We don't have to force things to happen. With this attitude, things that want to happen seem to unfold quickly. We grow more patient and trust life to do its thing. Before long, we *are* life, unfolding as it should.

New approaches start in the mind. Life happens *for* you—and *through* you.

--

No one is coming to rescue you from yourself: your inner demons, your lack of confidence, your dissatisfaction with yourself and your life. Only self-love and good decisions will rescue you.

~ Jenni Young

--

Three
Be The Cleaner

A peaceful mind is a powerful mind. This is a neurological truth. Your brain can work at peak capacity only when your mind is calm. When it operates from a place of fear or panic, you don't have full access to your genius. Peace, though often overlooked, is one of your most important assets as you work to get to the big leagues.

Linda: *"Onstage in my role as a public speaker, I enjoy engaging with the audience. I ask questions, foster dialogues, and sometimes take their temperature on certain topics. The responses help me gauge what's important to them, what they struggle with, and what might resonate with them.*

Sometimes I ask business audiences, "How many of you feel you have enough time in your days? Raise your hand!" That usually gets a chuckle but few raised hands. "How many of you feel you have enough money?" Louder chuckles, usually no hands. Then I ask, "How many of you feel you are loved enough?" More chuckles and smiles but still few hands because most people would welcome more love in their lives.

This series of questions creates an organic opportunity to talk about the three most common causes of stress: Time, money, and relationships.

Responses are usually predictable, except for one that still puzzles me. I always think this question will go over better and it never does.

"Who wants world peace?"

This should be a no-brainer, right? Nope. Always crickets.

Shouldn't natural human goodness prompt an immediate and affirmative response?

Instead, the standard response is confused faces and an eerie silence. I like to let the question hang in the air for a moment while they examine their minds. I can almost hear them wondering "Is this a trick question?" or "What does that have to do with anything? We're in business!"

Some may be mentally reviewing their investment strategies to be sure their financial security isn't based on arms sales or global wars. They're in favor of world peace but don't want to be seen as hypocritical. Others may appear confident that they're not invested in anything sinister, but they're still skeptical because they've been conditioned to see war as inevitable and peace as a utopian ideal.

"Who wants world peace?"

It's not a trick question. It's a wake-up question that leads into the next topic: War.

A peaceful state of mind is fundamental to business success. Yet we all fight battles every day, with spouses, friends, colleagues, finances. Social media is a natural battleground. Even our commutes are battles with traffic. We fight wars in our minds all the time.

When I talk about this, some audience members look intrigued, as though they'd never entertained the question but kind of dig its implications. Others chuckle as they recognize themselves. People approach me afterward to say that my loaded "world peace" question had caught them off guard. "That thing about peace really hit me! I never thought of it that way before."

I get it. World peace seems like a unicorn, something too good and beautiful to truly exist. But if we don't constantly and consciously work toward peace—within self, families, teams, and companies—the opposite of peace will win every time."

Mind Skills

The key to a well-functioning brain is to nurture and maintain a state of calm. Not lazy, sleepy, or indifferent. Just unaffected by conflict or fear.

It would be easy-breezy to have a calm mind if not for these two factors:

1. Human brains aren't great at distinguishing between real and perceived threats, which means that conflicts and battles you engage in, or witness, will send your brain into fear mode where genius can't operate.

2. Our minds can't be willed into calmness and clarity. The roughly 5% of your mind that's conscious is easily overwhelmed by your sprawling subconscious. Some cleaning up is necessary to attain a calm, well-functioning mind. You may or may not enjoy the cleaning process, but it's not a one-off effort and it can't be delegated.

Any leader who will have influence in and on the future has to operate with a peaceful mind in order to access their full genius.

You may be wondering why this deep dive into nervous systems and the subconscious comes so early in this book. It sounds complicated, and maybe less than fun. Okay, but believe this:

No fancy leadership strategies or managerial tools will work if your nervous system's reactions are overwhelming your brain's functionality.

Most people are constantly checkmated by their nervous systems, so we have to get our minds in order. Let's get on with a key part of the journey to becoming an impactful leader in the big leagues: Getting our minds sparkling clean.

1. Brain Roomba®

Few people like to admit to feeling fear. *Me? Afraid? No way!* When we say that our brains' fear responses are triggered by perceived threats (being left out, looking stupid, going broke), many don't even want to consider that their fantastic brain could have a fear mode. Let's put that notion to rest. Everyone's nervous system reacts with fear when threatened. We're not necessarily weak or fragile. We're just programmed to react this way.

The fear response sometimes is described as "fight, flight, or freeze." Physically, fear can give us extra speed and strength to fight or flee. Our bodies can even assume a "play dead" state to put off predators. These responses are how humanity made it this far.

The thing is that our fear responses don't differentiate between true threats and perceived threats. Being chased by a bear or reading a terse email from the boss elicits the same chemical fear dump and sends the brain and body into survival mode.

Fleeting moments of fear are okay; continuous generation of fear chemicals is not okay. The "stress cocktail" of adrenaline and cortisol wears us down physically, mentally, and emotionally. That's never been truer than now in this fast-paced age of digital information. Our nervous systems are flung up high one moment, and sent crashing the next: *OMG the news, OMG the stock market, OMG politics, OMG who died, OMG the client, OMG school shootings, OMG climate crisis, OMG the price of gas.*

Humanity is doing its best to evolve, but our nervous systems weren't built to withstand a constant onslaught of fear responses. Our brains need a lot of help to stop surrendering to fear mode.

When our brains are calm, our smarts can be in charge.

When our fear alarm is set off, our heart rates and brain wave frequencies go up, and an interesting change occurs in the way our brains process information. Blood flow and thinking paths originate from the middle and back parts of the brain. That's our survival brain, located in the unsophisticated hindbrain.

When we're calm, neurological signals emanate from the Executive part of our brain—the newer, smarter part in the front—and direct the rest of the brain's activity, even causing the blood in our brains to flow in the same front-to-back direction.

When we're afraid, our brains receive only limited information and commands.

Fear increases our chances of survival but diminishes our capacity to be strategic business leaders. When we are caught up in other people's drama and crises, or hypnotized by images of unfiltered global suffering, our brains operate at a lower capacity. When we worry about things we can't control or give in to negative thoughts, it takes our attention and focus away from the things that matter. Turn off the noise so your brainpower is constantly available to you.

And don't think you can skate by staying apathetic and closed off, not caring about anything. That's just a different coping mechanism, one that allows fear to trigger another part of the nervous system. Even when you play dead, you're still in fear.

All the dysfunctional coping mechanisms and stressors that rob you of your full genius are like dust bunnies in your brain, so let's bring out the vacuum cleaner. Here are some ways you can shake out the cobwebs and create a more peaceful neurological state:

- **Be diligent with your attention**
  Where attention goes, energy flows. If you give your attention to the negative in a situation, you invite more of it. If you pay attention to identifying the positive, finding solutions in a situation, and being forgiving, that's the energy you'll fuel. Are we suggesting that you go full Pollyanna, or put your head in the sand? No. But remember that the fear-triggered chemical dump is highly addictive. Don't let your automated chemistry be the boss. *You* have to be in charge of where your attention is placed. Make sure your focus is directed and re-directed at what matters for your vision, your values, your reason for being here.

- **Be vigilant about what you feed your mind**

  Good or bad, what you focus on will grow. Monitor your content intake. Lay off constant news feeds. Stop engaging in polarizing conflicts that go nowhere. Consider avoiding dehumanizing or violent entertainment. Don't play into negativity, even when it's veiled as joking. As the saying goes, garbage in, garbage out. If you feed your mind trash, you will think and feel like trash. You may be accustomed to the adrenaline rush that comes from these things, but that just means your system is protecting you by making you numb (and dumb). Watch, listen to, and engage with things that lift you up and make you feel good on the inside.

- **Practice having a peaceful mind**

  Find a practice that settles your mind. We wholeheartedly recommend meditation. It may take you a while to become skilled and to form the habit, but when you have, you'll be able to whip out that tool when you need it and get a huge neurological return on time invested. Meditating is like running a brain Roomba®. Just turn it on (start your meditation) and let it do its thing. Even the sound is like a mantra: *vrrr-oooohmmmm*

- **Remember your wholeness**

  You are a big, interconnected, wonderfully complex system of energy. Being your authentic self requires you to be at peace with yourself. Work at being consistent with your values. Strive to be kind to everyone, including yourself, rather than only to people who can do things for you. Honor all of you: The physical, mental, emotional, and spiritual parts.

When you adopt these new habits, you'll see an improvement in how your brain accesses ideas, solutions, and connections. This is key to leading in the big leagues.

But vacuuming doesn't do the whole job. Clean floors require mops and buckets too.

2. The Cleaning Formula

Our subconscious minds are mostly programmed by the time we reach the age of seven. Along with creativity, imagination and intuition, it's where we store limiting beliefs, negative thoughts, and voices that tell us we're unworthy, we're stupid, we'll never make it, we don't belong. *What I want is not available to me. I am unlovable.*

Nobody meant to install negative programming in you, but what sticks are your child-mind's interpretations of things you saw and heard from parents, siblings, community, and culture. You may have witnessed violence, felt lonely, been punished for missteps, or experienced abandonment. In a child's mind, these observations, experiences, and sound bites make huge imprints in your subconscious mind. Even if your parents never said an unloving word to you, other of their behaviors may have signified issues related to self-esteem or self-worth, and your nervous system carries that observation's imprint. Perhaps they had spending issues. *Imprint.* Derided or mocked people who looked different. *Imprint.* Said things like "Money doesn't grow on trees," "No pain, no gain," or "Boys don't cry." *Imprint. Imprint. Imprint.*

This programming is contrary to grownup thinking and causes conflict within self. We might say we deserve good things while feeling deep down that we don't deserve happiness or abundance. We may call ourselves successful and be proud of our degrees and accomplishments but always be waiting for the other shoe to drop. We may look at the people in the big leagues and think we belong among them until a voice inside says, "Who the hell are you to make it to the top?"

These limiting, defeatist voices are generated by the negative programs in your subconscious mind that dictates 95% of your reality. Unless you clean them up, you will exhaust yourself by fighting them with only the remaining 5% of your power and end up allowing the negative beliefs to win.

The notion that our current reality is dictated by limiting junk programming from childhood may sound hopeless. It isn't, so charge up your mental

Roomba® because we're going to give you a potent formula for deep-cleaning and reprogramming your subconscious mind.

It will take work to clean up and heal. You may need outside support. If you have a pattern of negative reactions, know that you can change it. If you feel stuck, know that you're not doomed to stay there. Everything can be healed.

Time to bring in the cleaning crew!

You are the whole crew. You're the housekeeping manager who noticed soiled, torn, or damaged things that need attention. You're the supply manager who provides cleaning supplies and protective gear. You're the stains expert who needs to figure out which cleaning solutions to use. You're the logistics manager who schedules the jobs. They're all you, so let's get to work.

The Powerful Reprogramming Formula has three ingredients:

1. Willingness

2. Emotionalization

3. Repetition

But first a bit more about how to find and reach the different areas of your mind.

The Cleaning Map

In this cleaning metaphor, think of your mind as having three areas: The conscious and subconscious mind rooms, and the connecting hallway that is your analytical mind.

Your subconscious mind is by far the largest influence on how you think, feel, and behave, These affect outcomes. Consider all the times you wanted to do or say or feel or achieve a specific thing, but no matter how much you wanted it and how hard you worked, it didn't materialize. That's your subconscious mind overriding your conscious mind's limited influence to dictate what happens in your life. The subconscious mind is the big room where your cleaning crew needs to start.

To get to the subconscious room, we first have to traverse the hallway of our analytical mind.

Imagine the analytical mind as a hallway with a big red door at the far end opening into the room of our subconscious mind. But if our brain waves are flailing all over the place, the cleaning crew can't get past them to reach the subconscious room.

How do we slow down our brain waves? By slowing down the activity of our minds, including critical thinking.

This advice may seem the most antithetical because businesspeople rely so much on their analytical minds and critical thinking skills. We've gotten ahead by being smart, thinking constantly, and always strategizing, so surrendering to a state of calmness may feel wrong. But thinking creates those higher brain waves. To clean up, we have to slow them down.

Cleaning up won't empty your head or diminish your smarts. Quite the opposite. You will clear away junk that has blocked your genius and stood in the way of your progress. Leadership responsibilities tend to bring subconscious programming to the fore, so there is no way around doing this work.

Using the Cleaning Formula

Now that we have the lay of the land, we can get through the hallway of our analytical mind to reach our subconscious.

Time to bring out the cleaning formula: Willingness, Emotionalization, and Repetition.

Not just one of those. All three. Can't make cookies out of only butter, right? You need flour and sugar too. The Willingness, Emotionalization, and Repetition formula creates new imprints in our subconscious mind, strong enough to override our old, unhelpful programming.

There is no mystery to identifying unhelpful programming. Examine your life and you will see what doesn't work. You may notice that:

- You often make choices that aren't in your best interests or aren't a good fit. You sacrifice your own needs and goals because of a strong impulse to please others, or a wish to be seen as selfless and kind. *Programming: Taking care of my own needs is selfish. I must please others to be worthy of recognition or love.*

- You stand aside when your turn comes up (in a game, for a promotion, on a buffet line) and miss great opportunities. You feel you are meant for greatness but somehow life always holds you back. You're afraid of failing or losing. You're afraid of upsetting the status quo. *Programming: I don't deserve good things.*

- You frequently regret your treatment of others. Perhaps you lose your temper and can't stop yourself from saying hurtful things you don't even mean. This results in a lack of connection and the feeling that you are constantly misunderstood. *Programming: I am a bad person who's not worthy of connection.*

- You walk on eggshells. You perceive people around you as close to breaking down, so you stay out in front of things, asking too often "Are you okay?" *Programming: It's not okay to show my emotions. I am powerless.*

- You always have to win, get the most, be the best, even at things that don't really matter to you. The only reason to appear generous is to make yourself look good. You must leave every encounter with a W in hand. *Programming: There is not enough to go around. I am not good enough.*

- You are consistently low on funds. No matter how hard you work, you never seem to catch a break. The moment money hits your pocket, there's something that must be repaired or replaced. And of course, any investment you make would be doomed to fail. *Programming: What I want is not available to me. I don't deserve nice things. Also, rich people suck.*

A shortcut to identifying patterns in our subconscious thinking is examining "absolute statements." Be on the lookout for words like "always," "can't," and "never." *People always let me down. I can't make money doing what I love. I'll never get my dream job.*

You might not like seeing these persistent, recurring thought patterns. They might make you feel ashamed. You'll probably resent the limitations they've placed on you. No use getting upset about it: You didn't choose your negative programming. It was installed during your childhood without your consent, and it's not your fault.

Doing this work is not about psychoanalyzing ourselves or assigning blame. We're just observing and noting unwanted patterns of thought and behavior. Look for recurring situations. List anything that comes to mind.

Let's each choose one of our own identified patterns and examine the unhelpful programming behind it. Believe us, we've got ours! It's time to clean it out (heal it) and then layer a new set of beliefs over the erroneous programming. A cleaner subconscious permits helpful thought patterns that can underpin our life choices and support our success.

Now it's time to apply the Cleaning Formula—Willingness, Emotionalization, Repetition—and start getting our subconscious rooms sparkling clean.

1. Willingness

The first order of business is to make it across the room of our conscious mind and reach the hallway of the analytical mind. The analytical mind is known as the "critical mind" for a reason: It's the first to call bullshit on anything that's legitimately out of reach. We have to be *willing* to make a new imprint that's in the realm of reality.

We can't make new imprints on our subconscious minds if we don't buy into them, or at least are willing to try.

The formula can work only if you're willing to recognize your negative patterns and buy into a new imprint. If a repetitive, self-defeating voice says, "*I can't believe you're still in this crap place. You should have gotten further by now,*" it brings terrible energy to our endeavors. We have to be willing to program over it with positive reality-based beliefs. "*You are the most successful person in the world*" probably isn't immediately achievable for anyone, so it won't yet work as a new imprint. But maybe we can believe "*I've done all right considering the unfair circumstances I'm in.*" It's good enough for now, and we can believe it because it's true!

2. Emotionalization

The second step is to try out our new truth to see if it *feels* true by connecting with our hearts and *feeling* into the new imprint. We want to find a truth that brings the highest possible emotional vibe without eliciting pushback from our Willingness.

The guiding principle is to find a kinder truth that you believe in and feel to be true.

"*Considering my unfair circumstances*" sounds like victim-speak. Bit of a downer. Let's try for a higher-feeling truth that we can believe. As our emotional bandwidth grows, we might think, "*Who's to say I'm not right where I need to be?*" When we feel our way into it, we might arrive at "*I'm right where I need to be.*" Peaceful and hopeful. Feels right, sounds right. Going from "*I can't believe I'm still in this crap place*" to genuinely buying and feeling that "*I'm right where I need to be*" is an energetic super cleanup.

Sometimes we try on a kinder and better-feeling statement and feel we've gone too far. If we're struggling with issues around self-worth, we can't immediately buy into a reprogramming intention of "*I'm super awesome!*" It won't work because we won't believe it. That's why the two of us don't unequivocally believe in affirmations. Yeah, we said it! When affirmations are used without first honoring our feelings about an issue, there's a counterreaction that leaves us worse off than we were when we began. Why? Because we don't yet *believe* that we're super awesome. Your inner voice would taunt you with eye rolls and sarcasm. "*Super awesome? Yeah, right. Who are you kidding?*" So rather than drawing affirmation cards with New Age fables about your fabulousness, feel into your space and only take steps that you are willing to take and can believe in.

You might move from "*I'm not worthy*" to "*Sometimes I feel my full worthiness*" to "*Actually, everyone has an inherent worthiness about them, even me!*" Great. You want to find a kinder truth, not an inflated lie.

3. Repetition

The third step is to repeat your new, kinder thought so often that it overrides your old, defeating programming. Take what you developed in the first two steps and bring it in. Use your intention to fortify your new belief. There are several ways to do this:

- Meditation and reflection

- Journaling and gratitude practices

- Behaviors and relationships that support your new belief

Use any or all these methods to make your new programming natural and instinctive. Get support if you need it or if you want to see more immediate results. The Willingness, Emotionalization, and Repetition cleaning formula is effective on most stains on the subconscious mind.

As stubborn as the subconscious mind is, it can't set its own agenda. It only follows orders, so you won't encounter any protests once you reach that room. The first challenge is in traveling that hallway of your analytical mind. This is the part of your thinking that will second-guess you and obstruct you from what you've chosen to work on.

Most experts agree that the critical mind is attached to our egos, the place where we're used to always being right and being smarter than anyone else. Understand that cleaning up your subconscious mind will make your ego smaller and your genius bigger. You will become more forgiving, more patient, more creative, more intuitive—all the things that the ego has no patience for. Your critical mind wants to protect you from being fooled, which is a good thing (and why this formula needs to exist), but the attached ego protests to avoid its own diminishment, not for the benefit of the whole you.

While you do your mind-cleaning work, try to distinguish your ego voice from your true-you voice. You'll receive a tremendous return on this investment of your time and energy. You will bring creativity, brilliance, imagination, freedom of mind, innovation, connection, big-picture thinking, creative communication, intuition, healing abilities, and consciousness to your impact, abilities that are sorely needed in the big leagues.

The Roomba® Swoop

The fastest way to accomplish the three steps of Willingness, Emotionalization, and Repetition is to practice meditation. It bypasses your analytical mind and doesn't stop to argue with your feelings. Repetition is itself the basis of meditation; focusing on your breathing or your slow steps, scanning your body with your present-moment awareness, or repeating a mantra.

Once your cleaning crew gets past the analytical mind and your brainwaves become smaller, your mind will know what to clean and heal. At this point, you only have to get out of your own way and let the automated cleaning do its thing!

Now you have the tools to use your willingness and willpower to embrace your kinder truth and have a more peaceful mind. Make that your new reality at a deep emotional level. It's a big job that starts with catching yourself when you think, feel, or act in ways that don't align with your vision of your better self. Identify the underlying negative belief and work your way to a kinder truth.

Being kind and peaceful will not make you less powerful. It will bring out your genius in a way you haven't yet imagined. People around you will feel inspired by your presence. We look forward to seeing more of it and you in the world.

--

"Our life is shaped by our mind; we become what we think. Joy follows a pure thought like a shadow that never leaves."

~ Buddha

--

Four
Executive Confidence

Many managers and leaders question whether the ineffable qualities of Executive Presence and Confidence are within their reach. We're here to help you acquire them and achieve what we call Executive Confidence.

First, let's look at a widespread phenomenon that undermines confidence and derails executive presence. We're talking about the focus on time management. In our decades in business, we've seen this approach fail over and over, and it's baffling. How did time management become so popular when it returns such bad results?

We believe that what we *bring* to the table is far more important than how much *time* we spend around it. We're not saying that time doesn't matter, just that there's ultimately no power to be gained from controlling your or others' time. And forget about having purposeful and effective impact on the future when you're watching a clock.

You might be thinking that time is a limited and unrecoverable resource. If every minute is important, why wouldn't we measure our precious time?

It's just a matter of priorities. What's more important: Time spent, or real presence? We've all been in meetings with people who are just "there." So few people know how to listen, stay focused, and be present that the same meeting has to be repeated again and again. You can spend time reading this page, but the words won't register if you're not "here" for it. Time is not the priority. Being present with the right kind of confidence for leadership should be the priority.

Before we can step into an executive role, we have to be perceived as confident. We hire people who come across as confident, especially when it looks like competence. We follow leaders who are confident in their vision. Confidence makes people feel safe.

But it has to be the right kind of confidence.

The wrong kind of confidence is a career-killer. Skilled leaders can spot the wrong type of confidence from a mile away. You know what we mean: The false confidence of a braggart, the brittle confidence of an imposter, the overbearing confidence of a narcissist.

Hitting the right note of confidence is a make-or-break skill that will propel you forward in business, so let's take a good look at it, including misconceptions, mistakes, new choices, and maximum returns. Relax your death grip on time management grip for a moment while we review the formula for developing and embodying confidence and attaining the coveted state of executive presence.

Linda: *"Stephanie and I first met in Stockholm, Sweden at the 2-day Executive Women's Conference. I was the Day 1 opening speaker, and Stephanie's presentation was the meeting's finale the next day.*

I spoke on the topic "How to Win in Business Without Losing Yourself." Business can grind the best right out of us if we don't pay conscious attention. We lose too many good people that way. And because burnout historically weighs more heavily on women, it was a particular honor for me to guide high-caliber women to insights and tools that will help them protect their own wellbeing while they make purposeful impact in the world.

That night there was a dinner for the speakers at the residency of the American Embassy, a lovely building on Stockholm's Diplomat Row. There was music, champagne, and Swedish delicacies. All the rooms were filled with powerhouse women, so you might think it would be hard to distinguish one based on her executive presence, especially because in business we're trained to act like we own the place. But someone lit up my radar on approach. It was Stephanie.

She had sought me out to compliment my presentation and I felt honored. At first we spoke about the conference itself and some of my messaging that had resonated with her, but our conversation quickly turned to the topics of families and other real-life things. We ate canapes from napkins bearing the Seal of the President of the United States while chatting about our New York City roots, our kids, the importance of meditation, what to see in Stockholm, old movies, you name it. My point is that even away from business, executive presence has a magnetic quality. It drew us to one another.

When dinner was called, the seating chart had us side by side, the universe's magnets doing their thing.

Now, years later, I've worked with many of Stephanie's teams to bring out leadership presence and collaborative qualities. Together, we make conscious awareness part of leadership's evolution in the business world.

The next day would be the first of many times that I'd see Stephanie present onstage, or even just enter a room. Her teams are right: She embodies executive presence."

Mind Skills

Let's examine Confidence and Executive Presence. Both come naturally to some people, and they don't have to consciously think about or work on them. But even if you're not one of those people, these qualities are not out of your reach. You are a big deal. Stick around and we'll show you how to light up a room and draw people to you.

Executive Presence Formula

As mentioned earlier, Executive Presence has two components: Executive capability, and an ability to be present.

1.   Being present (non-judgmental present moment awareness)

2.   Executive clarity (cognitive availability)

The first is more important, but it's also the one that's most often skipped by those who seek super-boss status. Combining our most sophisticated cognition powers with an ability to be present allows a heart-brain coherence that generates the essence of Executive Presence. Let's understand and practice both.

1. Being Present

Presence is a prerequisite for experiencing anything, in business and in personal life. We inherently know (but tend to forget) these things:

•   You can't be happy tomorrow.

•   Making money can't happen next week.

•   We can't change things that have already happened.

Our experiences, our actions, our emotions—good or bad—happen in the now. We know this, so why can't we just be present? Because something inside us argues with the part that knows that presence is what we want and need. Where does that voice come from, and why is it fighting us? Let's look at some uncomfortable truths about presence:

•   **It needs to be practiced**
    Presence is not a one-off like learning to ride a bike. It's a process that may initially require intentional practices like meditation. Over time, your life becomes your presence practice. Just remember that without intention your automated neurological functions will yank you out of

your presence.

- **It takes emotional courage**

  Presence requires emotional maturity and a willingness to be vulnerable. If you haven't done the inner work you will automatically avoid painful feelings that come up around the unknown, the unfamiliar, the uncomfortable. Pain is an energy, and energy has to go somewhere, so we transfer it either to our subconscious mind or to the people in our orbit. Both bring suffering all around. When we're truly present we can transmute and heal pain once we've felt our way through it. If we don't grow emotionally, we can't handle the hurt, or reap the rewards. Emotional maturity and a heart-brain connection are vitally important on our way to the big leagues.

- **It can't be cherry-picked**

  Presence is a constant state, not an ad hoc tool. You can't be absent in one area and still really show up in another. If you're not present at work, you can't expect to be present and emotionally available at home with your family and friends. It's too closely linked to our emotional and cognitive behaviors for that. Presence doesn't just kick in when you pull into your driveway or come out of the subway, because as the saying goes, wherever you go, there you are.

Neurology always has the last word. Our intellectual capacity will always take a back seat to our reactive brain and our nervous systems' ancient "safety first" approach, so be aware.

2. Executive Clarity

The "Executive" part of executive presence isn't about being the big boss. It's about maintaining unfettered access to the full brilliance of your executive brain.

Negative emotions like stress, overwhelm, depression, apathy, regret, anger, vengefulness, or worry close off our access to our executive brain, preventing us from leveraging the super-smarts that reside in the prefrontal cortex. A leader must, as Socrates put it, "know thyself," which requires us to understand and monitor our nervous system. That includes the subconscious mind and the different parts of our brains. Yes: Brains, plural. Scientists have determined that humans have at least five brains: The hind (reptilian) brain, the old mammalian (limbic) brain, the new mammalian (neocortex) brain, the prefrontal cortex, and—wait for it—the heart.

Again, yes, you read that correctly. The heart has been established to have its own cognitive existence, with a powerful neural network that makes it think, feel, and remember things independent of the cranial brain(s). Our experiences register in both, so the heart can be considered a separate brain that's interconnected with the other four.

In a strong, healthy, powerful executive, all five brains work together and strengthen the others.

Interestingly, the magnetic quality that "draws" us to people with Executive Presence has one more scientific explanation. Not only is the heart a part of our brain, it produces our bodies' strongest magnetic field—5,000 times stronger than that of our cranial brain!

When we learn to lead from the heart and use heart wisdom, we wield the strongest magnetic tool there is.

Your job is to maintain a healthy brain and find ways to connect with your heart. You'll be a magnet! You don't have to be all gooey but you do need to have a heart-based intention to make an authentic difference. Intentions of care, curiosity, and connection makes you a beacon of light.

Let's add the heart to the equation of Executive Presence.

Executive Presence Formula:

1. Being present (non-judgmental present moment awareness)

2. Executive clarity (cognitive availability)

3. Energy management (intention from the heart)

Presence Pointers

Maintaining presence is like dancing to ever-changing music, moving gracefully with the rhythm, adapting to each new song. Even if we miss an occasional step, we know we'll find our footing again. The important thing is to listen to the current tune, embrace the new beat, and go right on dancing. Here are some tips for your presence dance:

- **Catch yourself when you start to wallow in the past**. Negative memories, thoughts, emotions, and actions remove you from the power of the present moment. Be alert for feelings like anger, regret, shame, guilt, or vindictiveness, and remember that these reflect not just how you think and feel about an external situation but how you think and feel about yourself.

- **Don't let your mind run too far ahead of the present**. In business, it's easy to think that focusing on the future is the best route to success. But the world's energies, possibilities, and opportunities are in constant flux. We can't read situations or make good decisions if we're not present and connected. Anchor yourself in presence and strategize from there.

- **Notice when you check out mentally, emotionally, or physically.** Watch for feelings of cynicism or apathy, because if you don't care, you're not there. Only in presence can we deal with criticism, frustration, difficult people, personal crises, team conflicts, etc. Presence requires emotional courage. Sticking your head in the sand is the opposite of that.

- **Create space for your presence practice**. Find at least one practice that works for you and use it to nurture your presence. Linda's Mindfulness Intelligence program uses a number of approaches, including Jon Kabat-Zinn's mindfulness-based stress reduction (MBSR) practice and heart-brain coherence meditations. Meditation and other mindfulness practices won't make you abandon your thoughts of the future or forget your memories, but it can shield you from being emotionally hijacked by them. Presence is power.

- **Pay attention when you are in emotional discord**. Feel into the dissonance and identify the cause. Maybe you were confronted by a situation and chose hostility and rudeness instead of a more peaceful, caring approach. It doesn't mean you're a bad person. In fact, only those who are connected with their heart wisdom recognize and feel badly about their own missteps. Ask those you've wronged for forgiveness, and forgive yourself, too.

- **Find peace in being**. A peaceful mind is a powerful mind. Mental and emotional energies are contagious, so use your presence training to rise above discord and help others to develop their own peaceful minds. Remember, the strongest energy always wins.

Presence is the basis of your self-practice, but the real tests are in your relations with others.

- Can you be present and really listen?

- Can you be present even in the face of criticism?

- Can you be present when someone else is suffering?

- Can you be present to your own needs amid other people's emergencies?

Keep these questions top of mind as you move through life.

The Confidence Triangle

There are challenges to be faced on the road to confidence, to be sure. But they vary widely from person to person. Someone who's had a difficult life may relate to confidence differently than someone who's had a happy (or at least less difficult) life. Someone who fears having their contributions criticized—or overlooked—probably sees confidence differently than does someone who expects to succeed. Achieving the right balance of confidence helps you punch your ticket to the big leagues.

People who haven't yet done this work might think confidence is an either-or proposition: Think of Insecurity and Arrogance as the far ends of a triangle's base, with Confidence as the centered point at the top. Insecurity means low or no confidence; Arrogance, too much confidence.

Neither insecurity nor arrogance will fly in the big leagues, so let's examine them before we talk about next steps.

Insecure Imposter

The closer we get to the big leagues the more Insecurity can lead us to doubt or second-guess ourselves. *What if they hired me thinking that I can do stuff I can't? What if I say something stupid in a meeting? What if everybody hates me? What if I don't belong?*

Insecurity makes us afraid, and a natural response to fear is to shrink ourselves. We begin sentences with *"I'm so sorry, but..."* or *"Perhaps it's not important, but..."* or *"You probably already thought of this, but..."* Others will sense that insecurity and treat that person like an imposter. And if you've been treated as "other" since the start of your role, it's even more important not to respond with insecure imposter language.

Insecure people cannot perceive—or believe in—their own worthiness and value. Insecurity sets off a mind cycle of Doubt feeding Defeat (a deflated state) and Defeat in turn creating more doubts to feed more defeat. Only achieving an evolved sense of confidence can break this cycle.

Now let's look at the other end of the Confidence spectrum.

Arrogant Armchair Professional

It's easy to fall into the arrogance trap in the big leagues. We can't believe we didn't get here sooner. We deserve all the perks and the special treatment, and we would like people to tell us constantly that we're always right about everything, thank you very much. If we're not careful, our ambitions can be thwarted by our own hubris.

People who display arrogance to hide incompetence may be called "Armchair Professionals." These know-it-alls couldn't execute if put to the test. They form poor power structures in business and will power-flex by belittling others to maintain their façade of superiority. But like insecurity, arrogance also stems from feelings of unworthiness. The difference between arrogant people and insecure people is that the former drown out those feelings with ego noise while the latter cope by shrinking themselves.

The Arrogance mind cycle is vanity, ignorance and unearned certainty feeding a need for validation. It's why some bosses need yes-people around them at all times, and always sound so cocksure even when there's nothing backing it up.

The mind cycles of Insecurity (Doubt/Deflated – Defeat) and Arrogance (Vanity/Ignorance/Certainty – Validation) are alike in that both are painful and difficult tracks that see you giving up your autonomy and leaving your fate to others.

Things That Push Us Up

Mindfulness Intelligence can help us build healthy confidence and maintain our own autonomy.

Insecurity and arrogance are not the only options. We can choose a whole new way of defining and embodying confidence.

The word "confidence" comes from the Latin word "*confidentia,*" which means "in full trust." The Latin word-building element "com," meaning "together" or "with," may also have had influence.

Confidence is the ability to operate with full trust: Trust in yourself, in others, in life. But our life experiences have taught us not to fully trust anything or anyone. After all, sometimes even we haven't shown up for ourselves. Here are some things that make us more confident and help us operate "with trust."

- **Trust that we'll get up again if we fall.** Everyone has failures. We've made fools of ourselves and been mocked. But you can't make it to the big leagues if you don't take your shot, and you won't make it in the big leagues if a miss knocks you out of the game. And don't discount the value of the pause at the floor, either. Fall, pause, reflect, learn, rise. Once we embraced humility, once we learned to laugh at ourselves and move on, getting back up became so much easier.

- **Trust in our ability to be present.** We may prepare (or even over prepare) for an event and then use little of the material. That happens because things shift when present people come together and new information and viewpoints emerge. Only when we're truly present can we assess the room's energy and fine-tune our approach to match it.

- **Trust in our willingness to be curious.** We try to go beyond the "performance" elements of our roles (speeches, presentations, negotiations) and look outward. *What can I learn here? How can I help?* This always leads to *How can we do great things together?* Be curious. Ask questions. The answers will emerge.

- **Trust that we can handle criticism.** Leaders may be questioned, criticized, and sometimes even persecuted. Negative interactions affect the ego the most. When the ego is quiet, we can recognize good, helpful advice and remember that incoming attacks are more about the person who's issuing them. Build safe spaces within yourself and with close allies so you have someplace to turn when things go south.

- **Trust that the meaning of our lives is not dictated by other people.** We believe that what other people think of us is none of our business. We let other people be who they are while we focus on our own sacred connection to what we find meaningful. It removes much of the trepidation around any encounter or business deal, because we know we're doing the best we can with what we have and what we know.

- **Trust in the goodness of people.** As leaders our job is to bring out the good in people, not to indulge their worst selves. While you may encounter some bad apples along the way, most people want to connect and create. Look deeper for the goodness in others, trusting that it's there. From this trust comes confidence.

Does this noble list mean that our trust can't be shaken? No. But when we know *what* we trust, it's easier to maintain a trusting, confident position even in the face of trouble or tragedy.

Trust is an important part of making it in the big leagues. Leaders need other people's support in order to make anything significant happen. If we don't trust people, we won't believe people, or believe *in* people. Trust is key if you want to rise above insecurity and arrogance.

Top of the triangle

Being confident has nothing to do with being the boss. Confidence lets people contribute at their highest level, but humility is equally important.

Great leaders are:

- Humbled by the world's possibilities

- Humbled by the people and teamwork it takes to sees a project through

- Humbled by the knowledge that they had a part in putting it all in motion

Let's review how the combination of confidence and humility positions us for success.

Embracing humility allows us to feel a sense of awe and excitement even in the face of the unknown. We don't know the extent of our potential or how it will manifest. We don't know the exact steps to take to realize our vision. But once we humble ourselves to the unknown, we feel less threatened and become more open to ideas and feedback. When we accept that we don't know everything, we grow more patient.

Humility has a gentling effect on arrogance and insecurity and makes us more accessible and approachable. It opens our hearts to the idea of serving something larger than ourselves. Even though we can't always see every step mapped out, we can always trust in that bigger purpose.

People at the top point of the triangle are confidently humble and trusting.

Albert Einstein said, "The most important decision we make is whether we believe we live in a friendly or hostile universe." Your perspective is just as important as the reality, and your choice determines how your life will unfold. Choose to trust life. Live it with humility, curiosity, and confidence. When your mind and heart are open you can create meaningful change.

Things That Pull Us Down

Many things can stand in the way of developing our confidence. Things go wrong—perhaps several things all at once. Insecurity displayed as self-doubt or arrogance can reemerge at any time.

Some of the larger threats to assuming the right kind of confidence are:

- What other people think

- Overwhelm

- Humiliation

- Nervousness

What Other People Think

Fear about what others think of us is a common stumbling block on the road to confidence. Before we cast off that fear, let's understand why it has such a strong influence on us.

Travel back in time a couple thousand years. You might be sitting by a fire with your family, exhausted after a long, hard day of building, or hunting, or pulling up root vegetables to put away for winter. If your family was prosperous, maybe you'd been horseback riding in the English countryside, trying to avoid being robbed by bandits.

By then humans had been creating communities and surviving off the land for millennia. Everyone, even young children, had to work to contribute to their family and community. Life expectancies were short because pretty much anything could kill you anytime. Sticking with your people improved your chances of seeing another spring. Our most primitive conditioning tells us to care what other people think of us because their acceptance or dismissal could mean the difference between life and death.

We all have both historic and modern programming around how others perceive and value us. This double whammy of fear shaped us as we grew into adults.

Humans want to belong to groups and make great things happen. We are built for collaboration and co-creation. We need each other.

But our fear of being cast out is deeply embedded.

It's also not real.

Here's an example in today's world. Any fashion store sales associate can confirm that most people are insecure about their appearance. The customer will have the associate racing to bring more items, different colors, other sizes. The associate can hear them mumbling from behind the curtain: *This doesn't look right. I'm too short to wear that. These make my hips look big.* But if the associate asked, "Would you like me to bring you your size in the sweater I'm wearing?" there would be silence—because the customer is so invested in choosing clothes their tribe will approve that they never registered the most basic details about the person who's helping them.

You're 100% certain that you're always being judged, but the truth is that other people are focused on themselves. If they think about you at all, it's about how you make them feel. Your role in their eyes is based on their goals and needs.

It's liberating when you realize that people don't really care about your looks or performance. They care about their own needs. When you understand that their judgments have little to do with you, it's easy to place less (or no) weight on their opinions.

Less-evolved people will always see your existence only as it relates to them, while evolved people will make room for you, embrace your uniqueness, and let you be you. Secure people don't validate themselves by the appearances or performances of those around them.

Confidence comes from having a true understanding of our purpose. Instead of assuming different roles depending on the situation or objective, a confident person is comfortable in their own presence and awareness. They look for opportunities to serve or support without being performative or asking for credit. That's the kind of confidence everyone wants to be around.

If you trust that life has you in the right place, then the right people will show up for you.

Overwhelm

When it rains, it pours. A series of disappointing and deflating things happens faster than we can sort them out and throws us into a state of overwhelm. Learning to take a breath and regroup is vital for mental well-being—and for confidence.

When we falter on the climb to confidence, we automatically flail for the ego's favorite camouflages: Insecurity and arrogance. Systems that are already overloaded and flashing red don't need much to unleash a petty, competitive, or combative ego reaction. This is the time to be extra conscious and not allow the ego to react with insecurity and arrogance.

The trigger could be an unexpected professional setback, a frustrating argument at home, or a minor misunderstanding with a friend. Maybe a newbie at work comes up with a brilliant fix and we withhold credit, make a belittling remark, or claim a part in the success. Or a teammate's error creates a little extra work for us and we explode in front of everyone. If we stay conscious and remember that our egos are trying to manage threats in the only way it knows, we can use our more evolved functions and mind tools to stay peaceful and intentional.

You've probably been on the receiving end of subtle (or not-so-subtle) putdowns from people who are themselves feeling overwhelmed and threatened. Perhaps you've climbed far and fast, dazzling senior staff with your ideas and deliveries, and someone marvels aloud that you were the receptionist just three years ago. The remark is framed as *Look how far you've come! We're so proud of you!* but it's meant to remind you and everyone else that they're still in charge. Sure, it's irksome. But ultimately other people are not in charge of how you feel. You choose how to feel.

Humiliation

Humiliation is a powerful (and common) experience that can easily shock the ego into insecurity and arrogance. Some people even try to stave off humiliation by being the first to dish it out.

Professional humiliations come in all degrees. It might be a language micro-aggression. Someone apologizes for being late to a meeting and Humiliation says, "What else is new? You're always late." Someone has misunderstood what materials are needed and offers to quickly gather them. Humiliation says, "Okay, we'll just wait. You're never prepared." (Again, keep your eye on those *always* and *never* statements.)

It can certainly be more overt. When things go wrong in business and somebody's head has to roll, some people pick someone else to blame and lay on the public humiliation to divert attention from themselves. It's the wrong thing to do, and it ignores the fact that a bad outcome usually involves more than one person.

It's uncomfortable to examine the bad programming that got us here. The human ego will never have the maturity to want everyone to reflect on their individual and collective responsibilities and find healthy ways to treat each other and work together. The ego would rather just humiliate someone and get on with its day. People work hard to avoid being its target.

Here are two important things about this:

1. Teams and companies do better when everyone feels safe to reflect on mistakes and determine what lessons were learned.

2. Having humility is the best way to prevent or disarm humiliation.

Our egos don't want to hear any of that, but humility is key to confidence. Being humble means being okay about not knowing everything. It means not leaping to judgment. It means saying *You're right* or *I can see your point* and being prepared to admit when you're wrong. It's only your ego that struggles with humility. You are not your ego.

Being humble removes or diminishes many threats. Humiliation is one of the big ones.

Nervousness

Nervousness is a demon that can throw the best of us off our game and send us spiraling into insecurity. If this strikes a chord, please know that you're in good company. We know brilliant, respected experts who panic before audiences who have traveled and paid to hear them. No one is immune.

Right behind nervousness is that other demon, humiliation. Naturally. When we are anticipating humiliation, our nervous systems respond by sending out pain signals that are based on old experiences and unhealed wounds. Our minds and bodies respond to that threat in real time.

Those panic-prone folks we mentioned might not even know why it happens to them. After all, they know the material, they have notes or even a teleprompter, and the audience isn't going to heckle them. They know that flubbing a line will not end their careers. But the nervous system always gets to be right. Even when it's wrong.

While you work to heal those old damaging programs, find ways to calm your nervous system—breathing, humming, jumping—and remember that you can't win by pretending to be someone you're not. Stick with who you are, what you trust, and what you know is true. The audience will think *more* of you when you show your true self.

Stephanie: *"When I get nervous before a speech or presentation, it's usually because I'm overprepared and worried that I'm trying to say too much. In those cases, I step back from it and identify my message's three main points. I know that I can hold three thoughts in my head no matter how nervous I am! That calms me and gets me ready to go.*

But this rarely even happens anymore. Mind skills and presence practice have made it easy to feel the room's energy and flow and happily engage with the audience."

Linda: *"I get physically shaky when I'm nervous, and my reaction is* *like a big ball dropped at the top of a hilly San Francisco street. Once it starts rolling, it's hard to stop it. There are many ways that nerves can manifest, but this one is easy for others to see, so I've learned to arrange presenter aids that will help disguise the shakiness, like using a wearable microphone instead of holding a hand mic, and singing or even humming beforehand to steady my voice. I can even take advantage of the humming as part of a brief centering meditation before I go onstage.*

Preparation keeps the nerves ball from rolling."

Know what makes you feel safer. Remember that the anticipatory fear is probably more painful than the actual event would be. Keep your own mental list of things you can trust. It can help you cope with nerves on your way to Executive Confidence.

Trust your own resilience and your ability to handle criticism. Trust that your life is not dictated by others. Work toward trusting in the goodness of people.

Having Executive Confidence isn't about becoming perfect or omnipotent. It's about embracing what presently is. Use any approach that helps you find your way back to the present. Our guess is that you will find it near curiosity, gratitude, and joy. That energy will have you organically doing the things people want in a leader:

- You will appreciate people for who they are.

- You will understand people from what they say.

When you have connected with your own presence, you will welcome others' presence and they will welcome yours. Now you can be a top leader in any room you choose to enter.

--

"If you hear a voice within you say, 'You cannot paint,' then by all means paint, and that voice will be silenced."

~ Vincent Van Gogh

--

Five
Big-Hearted Boundaries

It takes a big heart to make a meaningful difference in the big leagues. The wisdom, authenticity, and deep caring of a big heart foster a good leader's ability to connect.

The case for heart-based leadership is clear and substantial, but there is a pitfall. A big heart can be vulnerable to manipulation and abuse, so setting healthy boundaries is key.

Linda: *"A client had landed a plum Managing Director role at a large multinational company. She was eager to make real impact and take the business to new heights.*

When she told me her plans, she mentioned that she wanted to establish a reputation as a "super-nice boss." I asked her to define that and describe why it was a priority. She admitted that she hadn't really thought about the specifics but that she's always wanted to be the kind of boss she'd never had: One who listened and cared, who was understanding, kind, fair, and good. She cited business articles that said empathy is an important quality for leaders and that kind leaders are more popular.

I kept probing and learned that she'd been in or around countless workplace conversations that criticized and mocked bosses for being uncaring or incompetent. Even relatively good bosses were given little quarter. My client had always envisioned herself as a kind, popular boss who people would say nice things about and want to work for. Anything less would threaten her sense of self.

As a super-nice boss, she kept an open door for anyone who wanted to talk or vent or just be heard. She quickly gained a reputation for being understanding and empathetic, and very generous with her time. She was happy to have their approval, but being there for everyone took her away from her own work, so she worked at home in the evenings and on weekends to catch up... until her battery ran down and then out, depleted by listening to people's complaints, hearing everyone's drama, and mediating their conflicts. The challenges piled up until she ultimately broke under the pressure. Doctors diagnosed it as "stress burnout."

The word "burnout" generally is used as a synonym for exhaustion, but when it comes to stress burnout it's eerily accurate. Stress "burns" the brain's nerve endings. Simple tasks like reading or carrying on a conversation beyond pleasantries seem impossible to execute, and focused thinking and smart decision-making are completely out of reach. This woman started as a high-performing executive and ended up losing pathways in her brain and becoming unable to perform even her basic job functions. Fortunately for her, she lives in a nation that mandates employer-supported health care, so she was able to access the resources she needed: time, and rehabilitation. Medical doctors addressed the clinical aspects of her burnout while she and I worked on healing her mind and heart and building out action steps for her return to her workplace. This time she would know that boundaries are fundamental to being a super-nice boss. She would have mind skills to help her lead with clarity, confidence, and compassion.

As an executive coach, I've identified two of the most common situations around boundaries: People who struggle to lead effectively while being authentic and big-hearted, and people who have difficulty setting clear boundaries for toxic colleagues and abusive bosses.

One more note: There's a popular workplace notion that "Our company is a family." No. Business agreements and family agreements are fundamentally different. Introducing sticky family dynamics to a business situation brings confusion, worry, and guilt that will contribute to bad decisions. If someone describes the company as a family, RUN."

Stephanie: "I've developed many friendships at work. Some have become my closest friends. Yet I still believe that being friends at work... doesn't work. I care deeply about everyone I work with, but business is business. We have work to do! If a friend messes up on the job, they will hear about it from me the same way they would if we weren't friends. This is sometimes hard to do, but the alternative would lead to much bigger disasters. I want all team members, the friends and the not-friends, to think of me as fair, a straight shooter, someone who cares about their wellbeing and their career development.

I try to operate from an internal place that aligns with who I am as well as with the company vision and team goals. But it's harder to stay in alignment when I'm under stress. Stress changes us, and not for the better. That's why I emphasize stress-reduction and mindfulness practices for my team members. It simply helps us show up better for each other. When I feel aligned, I can make smart, heart-based decisions while maintaining healthy boundaries.

That brings us to the topic of workplace socializing.

I value the social part of work life, but as a woman (especially in tech), tact is essential. Often a company outing or client function is me plus a couple of dozen men. I show up because I want to nurture relationships and feel connected to the teams and clients, but I don't want to stick around for the late-night, not-so-sober period. I nurse a Pellegrino and leave early.

In some ways, we've come a long way from the days of (all-male) boards and executive teams taking hunting or golfing trips—or even saunas—to discuss business. Clients used to demand to be taken to golf clubs. Offsites were held at resorts with wet t-shirt contests held at the pool. But in other ways, we haven't come very far at all. While businesspeople talk a lot about inclusion these days, they still tend to bond over a narrow set of cultural and gender-based activities. I deal with this at the C-level by finding meeting and team-building formats that circumvent exclusions. My go-tos are daytime events that allow everyone to participate and are appropriate for people of any role, background, or gender.

But sometimes you don't get to choose, and you just have to cope. A sense of humor helps. It certainly helped me on one particular vendor trip to China.

As usual, it was me and about a dozen guys. Our event planner had worked with the client organization to produce an itinerary for the touristy things everyone wanted to see and do. One of their wishes was to enjoy the "cultural experience" of visiting a Chinese massage parlor.

You're probably catching on faster than I did. I had envisioned a nice break for a much-needed back massage, so when we arrived I was quite overwhelmed. Instead of a peaceful, spa-like atmosphere, the place was huge, loud, and crowded. Like a Dave & Buster's for massage, but instead of arcade games and blaring TVs there were massage booths everywhere.

At check-in, guests chose the type of massage they wanted and were given clothes to change into. I went first, not wanting to hear what the guys chose, and was handed a pair of skimpy silk pajamas. Appalling. But when in Rome! I put them on and set off to find my assigned booth, peering around corners first to avoid running into any travel buddies. I can't even remember if the massage was good or bad, but the clients were happy. I chose then and still choose to laugh at the absurdity of it all."

Mind Skills

Setting boundaries is surprisingly hard. We want to do it but we also want to be team players. We may set them in our minds but then not police them because we don't want to be perceived as difficult. And if we set them and people don't respect them we'll feel violated.

On the flip side of this coin, how often do we cross other people's boundaries? How do we know when we've trespassed?

Boundaries are complex, but you can't make it in the big leagues without them. Your inner primer for understanding and setting boundaries operates on assessment of three key factors:

1. Personality needs and drive

2. Unhealed subconscious wounds

3. Consciousness level

These factors apply both ways. Understanding your own needs is crucial, but so is an ability to assess the needs of others.

Most people have some level of intuition, but these are complex concepts and our education in this area generally is poor, so we need to learn more and practice more.

You cannot succeed at boundary setting or in leadership when you make other people responsible for your social and emotional needs.

Think of your various needs as individual buckets. Every personality type, old wound, and current consciousness level has certain needs (buckets): A need for attention, or approval, or adoration; a need to be in charge, or to be right; a need to become offended or make angry outbursts; a need to be seen as lovely, or loyal, or smart. If those buckets aren't already full (healed) before you enter the workplace, you will unconsciously demand that co-workers and clients fill them for you. When that happens, you are easy to manipulate and boundaries will be overstepped or ignored.

Here are a couple of tricky situations:

- Leaders who want to lead and manage with their hearts (kindness, compassion, empathy) while also being decisive and effective.

- Professionals who have suffered previous attacks or sabotage from abusive bosses or toxic colleagues.

Our inner selves must be in order before we can master boundary-setting. If we aren't aware of and working on our personal needs and our inner wounds, we take things personally and are easily offended or hurt. When we raise our consciousness level, we find there seem to be far fewer idiots around us.

A study in the Harvard Business Review found that a whopping 75% of executives reported that the biggest drain on their emotional resources was "managing difficult people or office politics." We agree. Let's clean up, grow up, and get ready to show up for some healthy boundary setting and great leadership.

The Anatomy of Boundaries

Boundaries are about two simple things: What's okay, and what's not okay.

When we think about boundaries, we tend to focus on the "not okay" part: "*I don't like this*" or "*I don't want that*," but setting boundaries based on reactive negatives can easily backfire. Instead, use the Boundaries Formula.

The Boundaries Formula:

1. Feel into and define what *is* okay.

2. Feel into and define what is *not* okay.

3. Communicate both, with emphasis on the affirmative.

4. Communicate consequences for disrespecting your boundaries.

Once the formula's steps have been worked through, the emphasis is transferred to the affirmative. People are much more likely to respect a boundary that's described in the affirmative, because it doesn't feel like criticism or censure. *"If you get back to me before three o'clock, I'll turn your request around before closing"* is easier to hear than *"If I don't hear from you by three o'clock, you won't get a response until the next day."*

The "Not Okay" Trap

Another disadvantage of boundaries that are based on what's *not* okay is that they can make us seem rigid or off-putting. Negativity and limited awareness can throw us off our genius game.

You may not be okay with working weekends. That's fair. But you're part of a team and want to support your people and projects, so the occasional crunch can be okay. Your boss ought to offer comp time, but if they don't, you can ask for it. Requesting fair compensation is a reasonable boundary. That's why it's healthy to think about boundaries in terms of what's okay and what's not okay. It's okay to work an occasional weekend, but it's not okay to go uncompensated for it.

The Boundaries Formula works in more complicated situations, too. You could be presenting at a meeting and someone tries to undermine you by exhibiting disinterest, diverting attention, talking over you, talking down to you, or just being generally contrary. Any or all of these can happen in a single meeting.

If we're focused on what's *not* okay, we feel disrespected and humiliated and are thrown off our game. Our minds fill with thoughts like *I can't believe he's doing this again! Why did she say that? What did he just imply? If he doesn't stop looking at his phone I'm going to throw it out the damn window!*

When we give in and become annoyed, insulted, offended, or angry it generates resistant energy and negative emotion. We may feel invisible and unimportant, or think about giving up. A negative focus brings it on.

As author and teacher Byron Katie said, *"When we argue with reality, we lose, but only 100% of the time."* By the time our negative reaction hits, the bad thing is already happening, so indulging unevolved responses is to refute reality. Refraining from a response doesn't mean we're condoning the instigating behavior, or that we won't respond when the time is right. It means we don't exhaust our inner resources by arguing with reality in that moment. No person or situation ever changed for the better because of our dark thoughts. Honest, inclusive conversations about what's okay are the only way to change people's attitudes and positions.

The "Okay" Advantage

First, accept that thieves are gonna steal and jerks are gonna jerk. You'll encounter some on your way to the big leagues. It is what it is; they are who they are. The real battle happens in your own mind and heart: Focus on the other side of boundary setting—what *is* okay—and the mental game looks a lot different.

Instead of falling right into *"I can't believe he's doing this again!"* mode, your focus on what's okay can let you be amused. *"He's doing this again! It's his standard operating procedure. I should have put money on it."* Keep your resentment at bay, observe the silly flex, and chuckle on the inside. When you're not disturbed by others' affects or behavior you might even identify what would make that person less of a jerk. Sometimes people just need to hear those magic words: "I see your point," "You're right," or "Well done."

Your example of leading with light and integrity will always register. "Okay" lets you focus on others, hear what they have to say, and keep your mind open to any constructive ideas or solutions. Where focus goes, energy flows.

Let's be clear: Compassion and understanding for those who cross boundaries does not mean ignoring the misstep, but there's a time and a place to address it. Don't jump right to outlining consequences as threats, like *Stop doing that or you're fired.* People react to threats with the ego's fear-based survival mechanisms. Management through fear doesn't fly in the big leagues. It doesn't bring out the best in anyone, including ourselves.

Give people the chance to respect your boundaries. Be clear about what's okay, and if that's not sufficient, bring up what isn't okay. If that doesn't work, outline the consequences.

Use your big heart when controlling your boundaries. If your first reaction to a trespass is to take someone's head off, that's your ego talking. Ego arouses ego, so even if your zinger wins this round, they'll get you next time.

Research and evidence overwhelmingly support the value of heart-based leadership, but if we don't want to believe it our minds will find a reason against it. "That might be true at other workplaces but not mine." The big-hearted consciousness training of Mindfulness Intelligence has been tremendously effective for even the biggest skeptics. Managers say they can recognize a person with this training by their quality of presence and the signs of an open mind and heart. These are the people who can focus on what really matters, cooperate happily, and do important work.

Agreements + Heart

Think of boundaries as agreements between people:

1. Intrapersonal (agreements with yourself)

2. Interpersonal (agreements with another person)

3. Collective (agreements between people in a group)

In a work setting, larger agreements include having codes of conduct around litigious areas like sexism, racism, and misogyny. Policies are effective for communicating boundaries, but personal interactions can be a lot more complicated.

Healthy boundaries require that all levels of an agreement be honored. Certainly, important agreements should be discussed before they're made. A good leader listens and probes, because an agreement is more likely to succeed when everyone's input has been considered.

There are good ways to enforce agreements, and less-good ways. If someone interrupts you in a meeting and you snap, "*I don't appreciate being interrupted,*" the room's energy shifts, and not to your advantage. But if you connect with your heart instead of allowing your ego to take over, you might say, "*We all agreed that everyone would have an opportunity to speak, and I'd like to do that now.*"

If someone is dismissive of your ideas, review your own boundaries and remind yourself of their parameters, such as:

- *My value is not diminished by their need to push people down.*

- *My worth is not defined by their lack of understanding me.*

- *My right to belong is not dictated by their appreciation of my ideas.*

If those check out okay, consider broaching an agreement. "*Can we agree that these meetings are safe spaces for expressing new ideas?*"

You can't successfully set boundaries from anger or bitterness. They have to come from your heart.

Not Boundaries:

- Not getting your way doesn't mean your boundaries were crossed. Sometimes you will not get your way. No harm done (although your ego may beg to differ).

- Taking yourself too seriously, or being easily offended, are not the same as having your boundaries crossed. As Ken Wilber, the foremost living expert on consciousness, advises: Wake up, grow up, clean up, and show up.

- Boundaries are not about being right or wrong. You may disagree with the location of someone's boundary. They may disagree with yours. We don't have to agree, but we must show respect.

- If someone calls you out for overstepping a boundary, do two things: Apologize without "buts" or explanations, and get clarity on it so it won't happen again.

When Boundaries Are Overstepped

Setting boundaries is an act of care for yourself, other team members, and even the person who crosses over the line. Do people sometimes need to be reprimanded or even dismissed for their unacceptable or dangerous behavior? Absolutely. If it comes to it, you and your big heart can love them from afar. Buh-bye.

Those are big and important decisions. It's important to set and communicate boundaries from a mature and balanced place. Righteous anger is okay; vindictiveness is not. Be slow to judge and quick to forgive. If you're the boss and you believe the transgressor is coachable, get them the training and support they need. Many times, that's all it takes to bring out people's better selves. But if the harmful behavior persists, act decisively.

In instances of harmful or toxic behavior, hold your high performers to the same standard as the rest of the team.

Research shows that toxic work environments produce a tenfold increase in talent loss. If you want to work only with a toxic person, by all means, keep them and watch everyone else leave. If you hope to do better than that, remove the toxicity and create a stable environment so people can do their best work.

The threat of dismissal should never be used as a weapon or tool, though. As we've discussed, being "othered" is one of our deepest fears, so when our boss asks us to do something, our minds scan for the consequences of not agreeing. Our nervous systems perceive the survival threat and protect themselves by giving in. Bosses should stay aware of boundaries around using fear-based "motivation," and rein in any tendency to overstep. It's easy to say, "Well, she must have been okay with it, or she wouldn't have agreed," or "He's a big boy. He could have said no." But as we've discussed, the human mind is not rational. It scans for threats with the reptilian brain and reacts emotionally with the limbic brain long before the neocortex can arrive at a rational response. Everyone learning to fill (heal) their own needs buckets (personality needs, wounding, and consciousness levels) is the most effective approach to overcoming these fears.

Getting clear about what fits your Boundary Formula and identifying how best to communicate your boundaries to others is the place to start. Toxic team members must be dealt with, no matter how talented. If it's not yet at the point where that bad apple is spoiling the whole barrel, offer them a "detox" of mind and heart training.

Here's a cheat sheet to help you spot toxic people and behaviors:

Signs of Toxic People & Toxic Behavior

Most toxicity is connected to power. Toxic people's poison seeps (or spews) through their words and behaviors. We're a social and contagious species (hello, mirror neurons!), and toxicity spreads just like a virus. When that person also has power, their toxicity is magnified.

It's possible to protect against toxicity by staying in your awesome light, but even proximal toxicity can wear us down over time. The final measure we can take against people who resist training and change is to disengage and remove.

Toxic People...

Dehumanize by:

- shaming
- blaming
- bullying
- belittling
- ignoring decency

Power-grab by:

- stealing ideas
- sabotaging others
- never giving due credit
- trying to eclipse others

Destabilize teams by:

- playing favorites
- creating divisive work formats (unhealthy competition)
- talking behind people's backs
- conjuring conflict
- never, ever owning up to their mistakes

Hurt people hurt people, and healed people heal people. In the end, you may have to heal yourself by disengaging from people who will stay close only if you agree to accept their abusive behavior. Setting healthy boundaries is an act of self-care, love, and respect. You got this.

--

"If you're really listening, if you're awake to the poignant beauty of the world, your heart breaks regularly. In fact, your heart is made to break; its purpose is to burst open again and again so that it can hold evermore wonders."

~ *Andrew Harvey*

--

Six
Planted, Not Buried

A seed that's been poked into soil doesn't know whether it's planted or buried. Either way, it's surrounded by dirt and under pressure without any chance of escape. Everyone can relate to this. We've all felt lost, trapped, and hopeless at some point, buried under negative situations and emotions like failure, loss, regret, overwhelm, worry, grievance, betrayal, humiliation, or powerlessness. Hope can be found in the darkness if we think of ourselves as planted to grow and develop like a life-carrying seed.

Our growth will be determined by:

- The quality of our seed (what's in us)

- The quality of the soil (what's around us)

- The choice we make to acknowledge the opportunity for growth and be a seed rather than a dead stone.

Life in the big leagues will constantly remind you what you are made of. Choosing to see yourself as planted and not buried is pivotal to growth.

Stephanie: *"When I was growing up, I had no idea that it would be seen as a big deal to be a successful woman in the world of tech and engineering. At home I was treated no differently than my brothers: We all were expected to work hard and succeed. My dad is an electrical engineer and my uncle a mechanical engineer, so decision to go to engineering school and study electrical engineering hadn't seemed unusual.*

Imagine my surprise when I entered Brooklyn Polytech and discovered that I was one of only two women enrolled in the program! Why hadn't anyone told me that my presence would be out of the ordinary?

I once saw a TED talk by a woman who had grown up unaware of the fact that she was legally blind. No one had ever mentioned it to her or treated her differently, so she just didn't know—until she tried to get a driver's license. The folks at DMV informed her that blind people are not permitted to drive. "Wait, what? I'm blind?" My experience was similar. My outlier status was news to me.

It's interesting to be different, to be the odd one out. Sometimes when things didn't go my way, the thought would swell up that it was because I was the only woman in the group. Sort of an anticipatory victimhood. I wasn't sure I belonged, and it made me want to prove to the professors—and the guys—that I could be just as good at this as they were. Probably even better!

In my first semester I took all the basic freshman classes, including the mandatory Electrical Engineering EE101 class. It was a circuits class that covered power supplies, resistors, capacitors, currents, ohm law, and basic system concepts that would lay the foundation for our future learnings. Straightforward and pretty simple, I thought. There were only two exams, a midterm and a final. Nail them and you're good to go. Fail them and you're screwed.

I was chugging along fine with my other classes and considered the EE101 class to be relatively easy, but something was off. I felt the burden of being "other."

I believed I knew the EE101 material, but it was not translating to my grades. I had barely passed the midterm, earning the equivalent of a C. I was determined to pull it together and nail the final. I had more to prove than my knowledge of circuit analysis. I felt that I had to defend my right to be there; indeed, the right of any woman to be there.

On the day of the final exam, each desktop held a face-down sheet with the circuit we were to analyze and a "bluebook" of blank pages for our calculations. I had a fresh 0.5HB lead in my Pentel mechanical pencil, and a clean new eraser. The smell of productivity! I was ready.

When everyone was seated, the professor said, "You have one hour. Turn the sheet over and get to work."

I was eager and confident. I flipped the sheet, copied the problem into my bluebook, and began my analysis. Series circuits! Pffft! I got this.

Step one: Analyze the circuit by writing out the equations that describe it. Step two: Solve the equations to get the variable values.

My analysis went well. Within the first twenty minutes, I had the equations down and felt confident because once the analysis is complete the rest should just flow.

We all knew that exam problems usually were crafted to yield correct answers as whole reasonable numbers. I'd completed the hard part, but hadn't gotten the answer down to a whole number, so I revised. After another twenty minutes I still hadn't gotten there and I began to panic. My hands became sweaty. My heart pounded. What was going on here? I scribbled across page after page, starting over and testing my equations again and again. They were correct! My analysis was correct! What the hell?

Before I knew it the prof ordered "pencils down." Argh! How could I have gotten the analysis right and not arrived at the answer? It made no sense. And it wasn't like I hadn't tried! I had used up an entire 0.5HB lead!

As I left the room, I felt worried and deflated but I comforted myself that having done the analysis properly would be enough to earn a passing grade and let me move up in the spring as planned.

My classmates were chattering excitedly about the test. "Wow, what a gimme." "That was easy." "What a relief!" When they asked how I'd done, I didn't know what to say. "Well, the analysis went fine, but I couldn't make the numbers work. Was the answer a whole number?" No one would share their own answer, so there was nothing to do but wait. This was pre-internet when professors made you come back to the classroom a week later to receive your graded bluebook. I was nervous the whole week.

My heart sank when my bluebook was handed back to me with a big, red, circled 'F' on the cover. So much for proving myself. This failing grade meant I would fail the EE101 course. What a way to embark on my engineering training. I wanted to disappear.

But I had to find out what I'd done wrong. I opened the bluebook and found the wrong number circled in red and marked '-99 pts.' I knew it had to have been a big error because it that number meant I'd scored exactly ONE point on the test. It turned out that students were awarded one point for spelling their names correctly on the bluebook.

My mind and body were filled with anger and blame. How could the professor do this to me? He must know I know how to reason an equation for a circuit! It's so unfair!

I looked at my calculations and saw I'd had the correct analysis and the right equations. But I had made a shocking error when solving the quadradic equation. I had calculated 10 times 10 and arrived at...wait for it...20!

Embarrassment flooded through me, and my mind shifted from blaming the professor to blaming myself for this stupid mistake that would cause me to fail the entire course. Ten times ten... argh! Am I that dumb? I briefly contemplated dropping out of engineering school altogether.

I talked to my father about it that night and he was cool as a cucumber. I remember how much it comforted and strengthened me to feel his belief in me. "Screw them," he said. "Don't let anyone else define what you do and what makes you happy. Take the course again next semester."

And I did. I passed EE101 with flying colors the following spring and the rest, as they say, is history.

This early fail may have been my most career-defining lesson. It wasn't about resilience (although grit has served me well), or that ten times ten is not 20. It was about pacing, and humility, and not becoming blind to the obvious. I learned that I had to be present at every step and in every moment, without rushing ahead, no matter how eager I am or how high the stakes are.

In hindsight, I'm glad I was put through the humility wringer. I'm a straight-shooting problem solver, but without that learned humility my success could have been hampered or stymied.

After decades in tech, I can tell you that a solution's simplicity is what makes it powerful, and that it's usually the simple things hiding in plain sight that cause the biggest problems. Those of you who write code, as I did for many years, know that when you're too close it's hard to see why something is not working. You have to step away from the problem, return with a fresh eye, and go back to the basics. This holds true in all areas of life.

At the time I didn't feel lucky, but now I know how fortunate I am to have not just failed, but to have failed and grown."

Mind Skills

When spiritual thought leaders are asked whether growth comes from inspiration or from desperation, they say both are possible. People can grow through suffering or through divine inspiration, but humans usually will choose suffering. That's where the old saw comes from: *Necessity is the mother of invention, while desperation is the father of innovation.* We've got to be in a real bind to make innovative breakthroughs, or be in severe pain before we're impelled to change. But this collective agreement feels off. These are three things we know:

1) Evolutionary impulses pull at us to grow.

2) Our go-to instigator of growth is pain.

3) We hate pain and will do anything we can to avoid it.

Evolution's pull wants us to expand our human consciousness. It's taken billions of years for life to evolve from single-cell organisms to multicell organisms and then onward to fish, birds, mammals, and humans. It won't stop with us. We are designed to grow, to evolve, to play our part in the unfolding of the cosmos' full potential. But somehow, we still tend to say *No, thanks. I don't like pain. I can't even tolerate discomfort or inconvenience.*

This is circular reasoning. We want to grow but we believe growth comes from pain. We try to avoid pain because we don't know how to deal with it. So, when opportunities for growth present with their accompanying pain, we consciously or unconsciously pull away or change direction. In the area of professional growth, this belief system allows no true lessons to be learned and no real growth to be had, and both are bad for business.

Whether we turn to spirituality or common-sense truisms, we may resonate with Buddhist Master Teacher Pema Chödrön's wisdom: "*Nothing ever goes away until it has taught us what we need to know.*" Pair that with Albert Einstein's posit that "*The definition of insanity is doing the same thing over and over and expecting different results.*"

If we are here to grow, and difficulties don't vanish until we've learned their lessons and grown, but we avoid growth because it hurts, we'll keep encountering the same difficulties and reaping the same painful results.

Either we befriend the experience of pain, or we find ways to grow that aren't based on suffering. Otherwise, we're stuck and probably quite useless from an evolutionary standpoint.

The Light in the Seed

Archeologists sometimes discover seeds that are hundreds or even thousands of years old. Specimens discovered beneath the Siberian permafrost in 2012 were estimated to be 32,000 years old. They had never germinated because they didn't have the right conditions for growth. Scientists extracted some tissue and germinated a plant that grew, flowered, and eventually created seeds of its own. Yes, a frozen seed bloomed into a living plant when it was given the right environment in which to grow.

This is true for humans too. Even if you feel dark inside, a seed can sprout within you. That's easy to forget when we're loaded with stress, depression, or anxiety.

People tend to choose pain over inspiration as an instigator of growth, but if we open ourselves to inspiration, to feeling into our true nature, we'd likely find sparks of light inside us, kindled by the grand evolution of human consciousness. They are generators of growth, creativity, and innovation.

Feeling into our own seeds of greatness can be just the ticket if we can separate our idea of greatness from an ideal of perfection and a need for validation. Maybe connecting with our light is exactly what will make the difference. Even in business. No—especially in business.

If you're not yet ready to embrace your own light and greatness, the pain option is the alternative. If you choose this route, make the word *"through"* your lodestar. We've found some effective ways of making pain bearable so we can get through it and grow.

Let's look at the sham of perfectionism, the burden of regret, the prison of self-judgment, the freedom of self-kindness, and the gifts of the unknown.

The Sham of Perfectionism

Perfectionism pretends to propel us forward despite it being deeply rooted in the past and the heaviness of shame. If we're not perfect, something must be wrong with us. Until we understand that our need for perfection stems from shame, we won't have the tools for the healthy kind of striving and contributing that we really want to achieve.

The subconscious programming of perfection is "I have to be perfect to deserve love." Maybe our parents demanded perfection, or they rewarded us for good behavior. Perfectionism carries the implicit question *"What will people think?"* along with the troubling thought that only perfection can keep us safe.

Perfectionism is known to be one of the biggest barriers to mastering anything. Author Brené Brown wrote in Atlas of the Heart, "*In our leadership research, we have learned that achieving mastery requires curiosity and viewing mistakes and failures as opportunities for learning. Perfectionism kills curiosity by telling us that we have to know everything, or we risk looking 'less than.' Perfectionism tells us that our mistakes and failures are personal defects.*"

Members of marginalized, misunderstood, or minority groups may feel they have to perform at a higher level than others even though the extra effort may go unnoticed or unappreciated. We may think that a perceptible fault or flaw will take away our right to be here and that only perfect behavior can lower the risk of judgment or shame.

Brown goes on: "*Research shows that perfectionism hampers success. In fact, it often sets you on the path to depression, anxiety, addiction, and life paralysis.*"

Growing up, we were praised for our achievements. Getting good grades, winning trophies, and pleasing others was the ticket to approval and acceptance. In our minds, failure would have been the end of the world. Like others who received perfectionism in their subconscious grab bag, we know it causes pain and actually hampers healthy growth.

Here's an antidote for shame: Voicing your feelings and receiving an empathetic response can lessen or even banish shame.

The word "shame" itself seems to connote a bad moral compass, as in *Have you no shame?* Shame is often framed as a motivator. "Aren't you ashamed of yourself? Do better." Shame says there's something inherently wrong with you, that you *are* bad and didn't just *do* something bad. Parents do the best they can, but if someone's early programming says something's wrong with them, they'll carry that belief into adulthood, management, and the boardroom.

Shame buries us under the weight of a belief that something is wrong with us.

You can do something wrong and be corrected without it meaning you are hopelessly flawed. Mistakes bring up feelings of guilt, a signal that something needs to be made right. But shaming yourself or others into trying harder or achieving more is just not going to work. Shame makes us inaccessible for connection, without which we can't be good friends, citizens, or leaders.

Now that you know that perfectionism comes from shame, find a safe way to go through that pain by voicing it to someone who will show you empathy. Love will always win. Remember, *there is nothing wrong with you.*

The Burden of Regret

Regret is a painful state that makes us feel buried rather than planted. No matter how good a seed we have, regret makes for bad soil. Standard processing decrees that we should be punished when we do something wrong. We made a mistake and deserve to suffer for another five years. Maybe ten. The worse the crime, the longer the time.

Rather than accept invitations for growth, we devote time and energy to wallowing in our thoughts and feeling bad about ourselves. *I shouldn't have yelled at her. I should have fired him sooner. I wish I had spent more time with my family.* This loop benefits no one, least of all you.

Viewed properly, regret is a prompt for self-reflection and self-forgiveness. Be aware, though, that your ego will automatically fight it. The ego wants you to be hard on yourself so that you'll feel weak, because if you're weak your ego can be strong. Don't fall into that trap. Although self-reflection can bring on painful feelings and move you to take uncomfortable actions, we urge you to continue the work.

Realizing that you've caused someone else to suffer is itself a painful experience. But because it's based in connection and empathy, it helps you show humility and understanding for others who have erred. You might need to ask for someone's forgiveness. You can do it, but you should do it right, with no ifs, ands, buts, or maybes. Just "I am so sorry for what I did. Please forgive me." They may be ready to forgive you right away. Or not. Either way, your connection will begin to heal.

The Prison of Self-Judging

Our own harsh self-judgment is among our most persistent enemies. Humans continue to beat ourselves up long after a failure or regretted event is in the past. Choose a kinder way. There's power in saying *"I forgive me for judging myself so harshly."* Do it now.

If it feels too soon to forgive yourself, remember that until you do you'll remain shackled to the past, unable to move forward. Self-forgiveness throws off those chains and affords you a healthy, higher-level connection to growth.

Much of our self-judging comes from disturbances in our subconscious mind. Common programming dictates that we are not worthy of being loved or of belonging and what we want will never be available to us. We perpetuate this cycle by constantly "finding" new evidence of our unworthiness. But this is a mirage. Our minds will see more of anything we believe is a truth. Make a conscious decision to think only thoughts that fortify healthy beliefs about yourself, others, and life.

Life *wants* you to be well and happy. No matter what's happened in the past, you are worthy and lovable, and can achieve anything that is in your heart.

The Freedom of Self-Kindness

We can't be kind to other people if we can't handle uncomfortable feelings. We *want* to be kind, but then someone else is rude or mean or lazy or chews too loudly and we suddenly lose our kindness. When that happens, it's because we didn't stay loving.

It's vital to remain loving in the midst of pain. It's the very definition of compassion. We may unconsciously withhold our love for people when they don't agree with us. We may withhold our caring based on our own judgment of someone else's motives. On whose opinion do we base those judgments? Usually, our own.

Self-kindness is a primary root of compassion. Commit to practice talking to yourself in the way you would someone you truly love, respect, and wish well.

When we're kind to ourselves we're less inclined to assume the worst about others. When we're okay with not being perfect and not winning every single time, we can extend grace to others. When we let other people be who they are, we can enjoy the benefits of their true greatness—and they, ours.

The Gifts of the Unknown

When we feel buried, not knowing what happens next can be unbearable. We want things to change *now!* Even in a situation that isn't ideal, most of our suffering comes from our own thoughts about the situation rather than the situation itself. Don't blame yourself. Just as we're not usually conscious of our breathing, most of our thinking is autonomic as well. Our nervous system creates about 50,000 thoughts per day, only about 7% of them conscious thoughts. The other 93% are automatic, unconscious, or recycled, created with our limited human perception, tinged with our own interpretations, and stimulated by outside prompts. Our brains are like pinball machines that shoot out thoughts instead of balls. If we don't train our minds, it can get dark in there fast.

Mind skills can help us shift into quietude and tune out the chatter, a form of welcome surrender. Then we can explore and welcome what teacher and author Eckart Tolle called "isness." "Isness" or "suchness" is in the acceptance of reality. Not in a dismissive "it is what it is" way, but with patience and curiosity, being present to what *is*.

Moving through stillness into acceptance and then on to curiosity should defuse the notion that you must be in control every step of the way. You're not, nor should you be.

The brain's wiring changes based on how the mind is used. Thinking that we should be in control while constantly faced with proof we're not, wires us for fear and disappointment. Thinking that we should trust life to bring wonderful gifts and valuable lessons wires us for curiosity and meeting things as they come.

Feeling helpless or not knowing what's next can be scary and frustrating. The first step is to trust that you are made for whatever is coming and that you'll figure out anything that has to be figured out. That's been our saving grace countless times. We've learned that we can figure things out if we let them unfold in their own time, and that moving forward by applying force rarely leads to a great outcome. Sometimes it means taking things into our own hands. Other times it means just letting things be until they start to make sense.

At one point during the writing of this book, Linda made a videocall to Stephanie and found her covered in grime because she had just taken her dishwasher apart, diagnosed and fixed the problem, and put the machine back together. That's one (spectacular) approach. A few months prior to that, Linda's own dishwasher had suddenly stopped working. She ordered a new one and handwashed her dishes for six weeks while awaiting delivery, working the rote chore into her meditation practice but not doing her hands any favors. Well, surprise, surprise. The installer couldn't make the new dishwasher work either, until he found a wall switch that controlled the power outlet. It had been inadvertently flipped, cutting off power to the appliance. The old dishwasher had probably been fine.

Stephanie felt in charge by using her engineering skills, and Linda felt in charge using her mind skills. Both took the opportunity to laugh at themselves.

A broken dishwasher isn't much compared to the deeper suffering that we all encounter in life, but the approach can be the same.

An eternal truism is that this is a beautiful life that will someday end, and we don't know what happens after that. Nobody does. We project our fear of the unknown onto our everyday lives by worrying and by trying to control people and situations. We can let go of that when we acknowledge that it's really about the bigger existential fear: Will dying mean that we are buried like a rock in dirt? Or will we blossom and grow the essence of who we truly are with the sparks of Divine Goodness that form human consciousness? We don't know but we are determined not to let our fears control and choke out the beauty and the learning opportunities in our lives. As we embrace and befriend the unknown we can feel the gifts of curiosity and patience and a sense of adventure.

One thing we know for sure: You have greatness in you. Give yourself the nutrition of kindness, meaning and belonging, and before long you'll find yourself blooming again.

--

"Do not be dismayed by the brokenness of the world. All things break. And all things can be mended. Not with time, as they say, but with intention. So go. Love intentionally, extravagantly, unconditionally. The broken world waits in darkness for the light that is you."

~ L.R. Knost

--

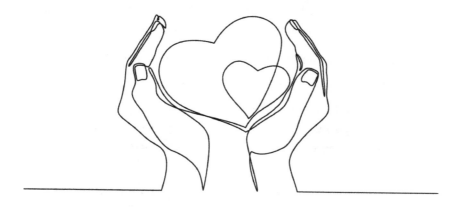

Seven
Grateful & Compensated

Those are important words. We all want gratitude and compensation. Lots of both, please! We list them in that order intentionally. Does that seem backward? Aren't we compensated for our work and then grateful for being paid?

In a Newtonian cause-and-effect world that might be so, but in the real world of people and feelings and money and energy, putting gratitude first helps grow the compensation part.

Some managers are always vying for the next promotion and another raise. The "push for more money" mindset influences everything they say and do on the job. They enter every performance review armed with endless documentation to convince the boss to give them an even bigger raise.

Others avoid the topic of money whenever they can. Many people are programmed at an early age never to talk about, let alone ask for money, even when they've performed a job or service. A teen mows a neighbor's lawn and waits to be offered payment. He didn't negotiate a price first because it would have been uncomfortable. They should insist on paying. But he can't ask, much less demand. He'll just be grateful if he does get paid. People can operate on this programming into adulthood.

Being well compensated for our contributions is essential to our wellbeing and success.

We work with and know many well-compensated people. They didn't get there by either pushing for or avoiding money. To reach abundance in compensation we have to understand the larger energetic reality around money.

Stephanie: *"I've always been the primary earner in my home. Fortunately, it comes naturally to me because while money is important it's never been my primary focus. I know my own worth and I expect my contribution to be properly valued.*

I've read that surgeons don't go straight at a target with their scalpel or tool because the human hand is less steady when moving along a straight path. Instead, they use a circular motion and approach the target slowly to reduce the likelihood of a miss or an accidental cut. This is an excellent metaphor for broader life. When we go directly at something we tend to miss the target. Straight-on energy can alienate people and increase our risk of rejection.

The theory applies when we consider taking a job that may or may not be great for us. In the past few years, I've observed a trend of executives using the "try-buy" system to find their next role. Instead of jumping right into negotiations for a specific role, they first "circle" the company, usually by visiting the office and hanging out with an executive or team, learning what they're about. If it's a match, you go to work with them.

I took this circular approach when I exited my first cable role after fifteen years at the company. A few months prior to my exit, I had felt impending changes at work. But instead of jabbing with my scalpel, I circled my network of people who know and respect me. I didn't know what the new target was, but not having a set target made me more open to just being in the flow of my industry and feeling curious about what might or might not come of it. My advice is to be out and about in your industry. Don't limit yourself with a set-in-stone agenda. Before you know it, someone unexpected will open important doors for you.

I was invited to meet with the chairman and top executives of a private equity firm that had made a recent acquisition. I learned later that an executive at the acquired company had heard me described as someone with deep knowledge and expertise in the technology and business model. I also learned that months earlier, someone in my network had had a conversation with the chairman of the private equity firm. It was just a casual conversation, unrelated to the acquisition. One comment—"You should talk to Stephanie"—had been responsible for the meeting. As I said, you never know who'll open that door.

If I had been focused on a specific role or a level of compensation, I might not have taken the meeting. I like making money but it's not what drives how I show up in the world. I am genuinely fascinated by technology and the leadership space. Call me a nerd, but I love that technology is such a big part of my life. That genuine excitement is why I take these kinds of meetings.

I already knew the chairman to be someone of great integrity and accomplishment. Contributing my technology expertise sounded worthwhile and fun, as long as it didn't interfere with my current job. I happily agreed to meet.

Earlier on the day of the meeting, I attended a luncheon hosted by WICT (Women in Cable and Telecommunications) to celebrate their Wonder Women Award winners. I left the event high on the energy of awesome women and headed to my meeting. As the elevator carried me up, I thought about the new people I was going to meet and the operation I'd learn about. Even after decades of doing business in New York City, it still thrills me to zoom upward in a skyscraper's elevator and take my seat in a conference room with sprawling city views. It just screams "potential."

The team, the executives, and the board had all gathered to meet with me. They described their products and services, explained some of *the challenges the company was facing, and outlined the vision for the future. The level of talent and brainpower in that room was spectacular, and I felt humbled and grateful to be there. My insatiable curiosity led me to ask questions about their tech, operations, and products, looking for hidden possibilities. They recognized my expertise and asked me approximately a million questions in return about the advertising technology I'd been working on for years, the players in the space, and how it all worked. I slipped right into my familiar "professor" role to answer. We diagrammed the advertising and targeting technology on a large sheet of paper to show how it worked and how it deployed around the country and the world. Two hours flew by.*

As I was leaving, I invited them to reach out to me with any questions, and honestly, I would have been okay if that had been the end of it. My expertise and passion for technology and business had served someone in my network, and that always feels great. The team sent me some good bottles of wine with a note of thanks for "making us smarter." Very nice. The end.

Except not. A few months later, and totally unrelated, I left my role at Cablevision. News of my exit made its way into the media, and the team at the private equity firm learned that someone who'd helped them at a critical point—and made them feel "smarter"—was suddenly free of obligation. They contacted me right away.

They floated the idea of my joining the company as Chief Technology Officer and leading the team that would move the company forward. That's when my instinct for the circular approach kicked in. Not so fast! If I'm aiming for something that I want to feel great about, where I'd be set up for success, I'll need a lot more information first. I suggested a short-term consulting agreement of a month or two so I could learn what was going on there before I made a decision. I wanted to see if it was a fit. I told the board I wanted to go to the Philadelphia office, where most of the real work was happening. They agreed and suggested I share my findings and feedback at a board meeting that was only days away. Ouch! Forty-eight hours to get a bead on a company and assemble worthwhile feedback? I was a little concerned, but I agreed. Mmm! I love the smell of Amtrak in the morning! I had only one agenda in Philly: to meet people and listen to them.

If there's one thing employees hate, it's when executives fall out of the sky and pretend to be a friend when they're really there to spy. I'm very aware of this and you should be too. No firm handshake or glib words will overcome their suspicion. They're afraid of being fired, moved, or demoted. They feel safer saying as little as possible. Imagine being in that situation: You already know there are issues at your company and the board sends someone in to ask questions. You do NOT perceive this as a good thing. Your defenses go up. That's what happened.

I set up meetings with the senior people, the chief operating officer, and the chief financial officer as well as the heads of IT, engineering, and technical operations. All seemed suspicious of me. But I understood. I met them with empathy. As a consultant, I had no agenda beyond finding out the truth, and as usual, my curiosity kicked in. I was genuinely interested in what they had to say. My open-minded, open-hearted energy was clear in my questions. "How are you doing? Do you have what you need from management? Do you feel supported? Why do you think things are perceived as not working optimally?" They could identify my stance from the nuances of my queries. I purposely used the word "perceived" because I wasn't there to run someone else's play. I wanted them to know that I wasn't laying blame or insinuating anything. I had candid, open conversations with several team members. I asked for their opinions and absorbed them all.

Even though my fact-finding mission had gone even better than I'd expected, while on the train back to New York City I recognized that I felt stressed. I was combing through my notes to figure out what to present to the board the next morning when I would meet the newly hired chief revenue officer. My engineering mind always wants to identify the problem and either solve it or find a workaround. This assignment had no such space. I had only my observations, and it would have to be enough.

After a really brilliant presentation from the new CRO, it was my turn. I had only a single sheet of notes and made the rookie mistake of opening with an apology: "I was only there for twenty-four hours, so..." I caught myself and quickly corrected my approach. I told them that they had some specific technical and operational challenges that prevented teams from generating reports quickly enough to leave time for needed changes. "It's like flying the Starship Enterprise toward a mountain range without a working altimeter," I told them. Well, not everyone is a sci-fi nerd. I saw a lot of confused expressions, so I explained that the slowness of the data feedback loop was impairing the business and its ability to scale. I offered some recommendations and suggestions before leaving. Aside from the nice consulting fee I'd receive for this gig, my intention was to help, and I was satisfied.

They soon called to reiterate the CTO offer, and this time it was easy to say yes. I knew what I'd be getting myself into. Now the compensation discussion was easy. It's not primarily about the money. I don't look for jobs; I look for positions that I'll find fulfilling. Being genuinely excited about what you do is as key as having the intention to help. I had agreed to help someone important to me and it led to an almost six-year stint as the company's CTO and CTO/COO before I moved into a CTO role at a Fortune 100 company.

It all started with 'Sure, I'd love to help.'"

Linda: *"I have coached a few recruiters and am always baffled at the things that make or break candidates. You'd think it would be salary, responsibilities, or reporting structure. But no. As with most things in business, in the end, it has very little to do with business.*

A client who worked on a hiring company's side told me about a person who had long sought a senior position and had turned up as a great candidate for a Managing Director role with a six-figure salary.

Recruiting processes for senior positions are extensive, entailing numerous interviews, but this candidate did well and was shortlisted and ultimately selected. All that remained was the negotiation, which should have been routine. The job's salary level and most other elements had been established and communicated during the interview process.

But not this guy. As soon as he received the good news, he asked for a significant bump in the offered salary. He was told it was too late in the game to adjust and there would be future opportunities to revisit it. What they were really saying was that he shouldn't have pursued the job if he had thought the salary was too low.

This sort of thing raises the ire—and the defenses—of a hiring manager. Consciously or unconsciously, they feel at best annoyed; at worst betrayed. He waited until now to ask for more? Who is this guy to ignore normal protocols? What other codes of conduct will he flout? Does he understand the nature of our industry and the market? Do we really want him in a leadership position?

When he failed to get the offer bumped up, he did what most people do when they take this sort of thing personally: He went hard after smaller things, asking for a relocation package in the high five figures. His ego—dressed as greed—was out of the cage. If his concern really had been having his moving costs covered, he could have asked that the company arrange and pay for the movers, Realtor fees, closing costs, whatever. But it wasn't really about any of that. He was trying to soothe his bruised ego the way the ego wants him to: By aggressively going after more, more, more.

He continued to dig in his heels as his ego donned another favorite guise: Saboteur. After he'd made it through a long job search and a lengthy hiring process, he refused to budge on the relocation package.

The company had seen enough. The offer was rescinded.

Letting his ego run unchecked set back his own career trajectory and wasted the recruiter's and company's time and resources. All he needed was to have had a few drops of gratitude for the opportunity to join a great company and be well compensated. If only he'd trained his mind to reroute to a more constructive path."

Mind Skills

As we prepared to write this book, we made it our mission to understand what has brought us great compensation and what hasn't, and to examine the factors that make us want to generously compensate our own employees.

We kicked around words like "helpful," "loyal," "confident," and "consistent" but kept coming back to "gratitude." Not being thankful for scraps, but a genuine appreciation for the possibilities that come out of projects and relationships. We concluded that a state of gratitude plays the biggest part on both sides of the table.

The American Psychological Association defines gratitude as a "sense of happiness and thankfulness in *response* to a fortunate happenstance or tangible gift." We respect this definition, but we find a suggested reactiveness in the word "response" that we don't think does justice to the power of gratitude.

Gratitude can be conjured before the desired outcome has been achieved, and it increases the chance of success. The world is a big flow of energy, and there is an energy to great things, things that we're happy and excited about, things that make us feel alive. Gratitude aligns with that energy. When we assume gratitude even before our dream or goal has manifested, we are vibing on that wavelength.

When it comes to energy like attracts like. The things we vibe with find us.

Think about round pegs and square holes. Positive things, including gratitude, are round holes. When we feel gratitude, we become round pegs that fit perfectly into those great things. You can try to jam a square peg into a round hole, just as you can *try* to be an inspiring leader when you're feeling angry or resentful, but a square peg can't fit into a round hole. Even brute force won't work. It will just exhaust you, and could destroy the apparatus too.

Gratitude is good for you all around. A study of therapy patients had one group write letters of gratitude while another group journaled about negative experiences they'd had. Those who wrote letters of gratitude felt better and recovered sooner, while those who journaled reported feelings of anxiety and depression. [*Y. Joel Wong, Jesse Owen, Nicole T. Gabana, Joshua W. Brown, Sydney McInnis, Paul Toth & Lynn Gilman (2018) Does gratitude writing improve the mental health of psychotherapy clients? Evidence from a randomized controlled trial, Psychotherapy Research, 28:2, 192-202, DOI: 1 0.1080/10503307.2016.1169332*].

That on which we focus grows.

Gratitude is remarkable.

People who feel and express gratitude have a higher volume of grey matter in their brains [Zahn R, Garrido G, Moll J, Grafman J. *Individual differences in posterior cortical volume correlate with proneness to pride and gratitude.* Soc Cogn Affect Neurosci. 2014 Nov;9(11):1676-83]. The human brain contains about 86 billion neurons. They allow your brain to process and produce information and control movement, memory, and emotions. Increased grey matter is increased brain power.

At the neurochemical level, feelings of gratitude are associated with an increase in neural modulation of the prefrontal cortex. That's the "executive" part of the brain that's responsible for attention, impulse inhibition, prospective memory, cognitive flexibility, and for managing negative emotions like guilt, shame, and aggression.

Unsurprisingly, research shows that gratitude improves all interpersonal relationships, both at work and at home [Gordon, A. M., Impett, E. A., Kogan, A., Oveis, C., & Keltner, D. (2012). *To have and to hold: Gratitude promotes relationship maintenance in intimate bonds.* Journal of Personality and Social Psychology, 103(2), 257–274]. We've all felt—from both sides—the benefits of sincere appreciation and a heartfelt "Thank you."

There's also a clear connection between gratitude and good health. Research shows that keeping a gratitude journal can diminish stress, improve the quality of sleep, and build emotional awareness. Adding verbal and behavioral expressions of gratitude enhances our own positivity and makes us more empathetic.

If you're really honest about it, money itself probably isn't the primary goal in your work life. It's how you think the money will make you feel: Appreciated, recognized, influential, powerful, safe. If you were collecting a big paycheck from an abusive boss, would you wish for more money? No. You'd wish for a better job.

Imagine what gratitude can do for you on your mission to find the dream job that will compensate you abundantly. You'd be more likely to be perceived as helpful, magnetic, effective, emotionally aware, and serene even in the face of stress or negativity. That's top-candidate stuff.

Here's a fun gratitude exercise. Let's take a trip into the future and reflect on your life. That perspective is helpful because we tend to overestimate what we can do in a year but underestimate what we can accomplish in a decade.

It's ten years from now and you are at an awards event. You've just been announced as the winner. What is the award for? Why were you chosen? What wonderful things did the presenter say about you? Write down what you dream of hearing. It can be brief or lengthy. It's your future! You decide.

Now you are onstage to accept your award. Who will you thank in your speech? What are you grateful for that helped you to get here? Write down what you would love to say. Lastly, as you imagine this scene: How do you feel? Don't just write it down, feel it! That's golden energy right there.

Remember, you can summon gratitude anytime. It's just a matter of choosing where to place your focus.

From the Other Side of the Table

As employers, we know that people who live at the grateful end of the spectrum make better workers and leaders and are much more pleasant to be around. When hiring, we look for a gratitude vibe. It augurs well for what's to come.

Science backs us up: Grateful workers are more efficient, more productive, and more responsible. Expressions of gratitude in the workplace build interpersonal bonds and trigger feelings of closeness [Algoe, S., *Find, Remind, and Bind: The Functions of Gratitude in Everyday Relationships*, Social and Personality Compass, 2012: Vol 6, Issue 6, 455-469]. People who practice grateful behaviors at work volunteer for more assignments, go further to accomplish tasks, and work happily as a part of a team.

Managers and supervisors who feel and express gratitude maintain a stronger group cohesiveness, with better productivity.

Anyone who's sat in the hiring chair has had experiences with great candidates and disastrous ones. Employers look for people who have the talent, expertise, experience, and leadership skills to successfully do the job, but they also judge them consciously, unconsciously, or both. *"I just didn't like him"* is a common reason that an offer is not extended. An attitude of gratitude helps you.

When it's time to ask for a raise, know that the past is the past. Salary bumps aren't usually given for previous performance. You did the job you were paid to do. Raises are given based on what's expected of you now. Don't go to that meeting with a list of your accomplishments. Be proud of them, sure, but it's more important to be ready to explain what you think went well and why, what you might have done differently, and how you're going to contribute going forward.

Remember your gratitude. Don't start sentences with "I," "Me," or "My" when credit is being handed out. Don't begin an explanation of something that went wrong with "He," "She," or "They." Bosses want to see in you a person who understands the interconnected process of business success and is able to self-reflect and reevaluate. A self-aware team player is the golden goose. Overall they're focused on future success, what you want to achieve, and how you plan to do it.

Money Triggers

"Money" is a small word but carries a ton of energy from the meaning we place on it. It would take another book to describe all the varieties of generational conditioning around money. But money itself is neutral. It has no inherent meaning. It's just a thing we trade for other things. Granted, a lot of them are important things like food, clothing, and shelter. But the importance we place on money goes beyond logic.

Money has shifted from being a tool for security to a psychological marker of power—or the lack thereof.

Money's measurable nature leads to the erroneous belief that salary reflects our own value. Being turned down for a raise can seem like a personal rejection. You feel dismissed and disempowered. Something in the darkness of your subconscious mind whispers that you are not worthy, that universal fear that's so deeply embedded in human programming.

Even as adults, dealing with other adults, childhood money triggers remain. As an employer, you're effectively dealing with children who seek healing and validation from the level of compensation you award them. Your own programmed money triggers are in the mix too. If you don't stay mindful of this, you are likely to make unnecessary mistakes.

- You might not do a great job of hiding your impatience with an employee's salary demands. Your whole demeanor says "It's just business. Take your damn paycheck and go cry somewhere else." Even if you don't say it out loud, it's felt, and it could create a grudge in the employee somewhere between quiet quitting and active sabotage.

- Perhaps you've had enough of an employee's self-promoting behavior and show them the exit. There goes your return on the cost of finding, hiring, training, and compensating them. Here comes the cost of replacing them too.

- Maybe you, like countless leaders, underestimate how much it means to an employee to receive sincere appreciation, to be seen and heard, and to be supported on their development path. Remember, being a mensch costs nothing.

It's never just about the money, no matter what our triggers tell us, or what people say in a negotiation process.

It's easy to spot people who overcompensate for a self-perceived "unworthiness" by going overboard on the chest-pounding. They make a big Me-deal out of things and need constant validation. *My senior title is who I am. Being a high earner is how I define myself. Being the project lead is my birthright.* Sure, self-involved people are irritating, but they have those worthiness issues. Be sure to communicate your respect for them. You'll be supporting their leadership potential and giving them something much more valuable than money if you can get them to buy into the idea of serving a larger goal, or even stepping aside to let others grow.

It's a little trickier to identify the people who won't ask for the compensation they deserve. They feel underappreciated and underpaid, but their unworthiness programming tells them that asking for what they want is not safe and their nervous system shuts down. It just won't go there. It responds with *If they think I'm worth more, they should offer me more.* This leads to hurt feelings, grudges, and general negativity. Pay attention, because the loyal people who don't ask for much are more likely to burn out.

Stubborn self-worth conditioning makes it difficult to create or achieve some of the most important things in work life: A place that values and nurtures our talent; compensation that covers our needs and makes us feel appreciated; and a sense of meaning and belonging. Those things happen only for emotionally healthy people. The emotional state of gratitude helps us heal in all areas of life.

Pursuing a New Role

In the run-up to any interview, do your homework first. Learn everything you can about the organization and the people who'll be interviewing you. Even the most senior people love to have their contributions and value acknowledged by others, and they'll like you more for it.

If all goes well and you're a fit for the position (or the company is willing to create a position that fits you), think about your planned arc, including what the end of the gig will look like. It might sound counterintuitive or even aggressive to talk about the end at the beginning, but not knowing the parting terms puts you at a disadvantage, now and down the road.

- If you don't know what will happen at exit time, it's harder to negotiate appropriate compensation.

- Your job performance can be affected by concerns over the unknown consequences of a sudden parting.

That's why you should have the discussion up front about severance and what constitutes a trigger of the terms. It makes it easier to pinpoint compensation on all other levels: length of the engagement, salary, bonus, health benefits, vacation days, personal days, and even the matter of how expenses are covered. That's important because having the company cover things like travel, vehicles, insurance, phone service, and subscriptions means fewer out-of-pocket expenditures for you and less administrative work to do for reimbursement. Calculate and ask for a stipend to cover continuing education and network memberships. Nothing takes you higher than continuing to learn and grow and network. And if the company offers private jets and car services, get clarity on the level of access you'll have.

Work-from-home is a key issue now, especially for those in midlevel positions with less autonomy. Ask for what you need, but in any big-league situation, it's best to show up in person as often as you can. As a leader and energy-setter, honor the value of being in the room.

Ace It

The best part of a good agreement is that it sets the stage for you to feel good and start delivering from Day One. Be sure to get the comp that your contribution is worth and the extras that will set you up for success.

Find The Right Level:

- Know the worth of the position. Talk to people in your network to gauge the range for similar roles.

- Women! Minorities! Know your actual worth. Find out what a white man in the role would make.

- Make every effort to learn what your predecessor was getting.

- If the number your research leads to is much higher than your current comp, ask for it anyway. Chances are that you're being underpaid.

- Never, ever answer questions about the compensation you received in a previous position.

Set Yourself Up for Success:

- Don't wait until you've been onboarded to ask for what you need to be successful.

- Get a good read of the company from the top: Its vision, mission, and values – and look for signs that they are lived.

- Meet the people who will be your direct reports.

- Try to get a read on the company from those already in place.

- Learn the company culture.

- Understand the organization, budgets, and resources.

- Confirm that the senior team will support you and your ideas.

- Identify what worked and didn't work when your predecessor was in the role.

- Know what's expected of you.

- Find out what kind of education and support are available to you and your teams.

- Clearly communicate the value you'll bring to the role and company— and be clear about what you'll need for success.

Do you really need to do all these things? Yes, you do, and before you sign on the dotted line.

Lay out a clear map and feel into your findings before you decide whether this position is right for you. How can you inspire your staff to greatness if you are not aligned with the company's purpose and the leadership vibe? How will you accomplish anything significant if you are mired in endless office politics? How can you live up to high expectations without the proper resources?

Ask these questions and listen to the answers, spoken and unspoken. Healthy organizations with good agendas and environments will intersect with your own objectives. If what you learn feels good to you, you're positioned for success.

Having gratitude during the process of seeking a fulfilling role, making conscious impact, and being generously compensated isn't about being a softie. Gratitude makes us better and improves the way our brains work. Gratitude expands your ability to stay calm and emotionally connect with people. Gratitude can also prevent you from being triggered into making mistakes in the negotiation process. Gratitude makes you more powerful.

If you've fallen just short of goals, or been flat-out rejected for your dream job, remember "rejection" can also mean "protection" or "redirection."

Some jobs are not meant for you. You wouldn't even want them if you knew more about them. That's why it's so important to know how you want to feel in your new position and what it will take to make you feel that way. It might be a certain level of autonomy, creative decision-making opportunities, earning at a level that opens new doors, or working with people who care about the company and its success as much as you do. These things are much more likely to become reality if you first do the homework and then thank the universe for making it happen.

The more you live in the energy of those wishes, the more likely it is that they'll manifest.

It's fun to operate in the big leagues with a platform that can further your impact on the world. It can be exhausting, though, because now the stakes are higher and you're a larger projection surface, so be sure to find ways to take care of yourself mentally, emotionally, and spiritually. The big leagues are worth it.

--

"Walk as if you are kissing the Earth with your feet."
~ Thich Nhat Hanh

--

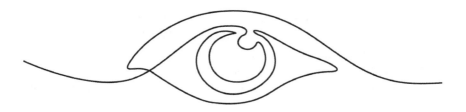

Eight
Room Reader with a Bullshit Radar

Everyone has awful moments in their professional life: A bad deal, a poor decision, a regrettable hire, a public humiliation—even our own firing. Sometimes, as angry, disappointed, or hurt as we may be, the worst part is the feeling that we should have known better. The situation might have been avoided or mitigated had we read the room better or spoken out at the first sign of a problem.

Linda: "As CEO of a branding agency, I was always looking for ways to expand the business. We implemented an investment track so we could put money and design services behind new or smaller brands that couldn't afford to hire us. Smart bets would produce higher returns, and as shareholders, we would encounter little interference in the creative process and produce award-winning designs.

That was the idea, anyway.

A local wellness spa had been getting buzz for its massage treatments and organic products. It was co-owned by a one-hit-wonder former popstar and a super-crunchy introvert.

The place itself was lovely, reminiscent of an old apothecary shop, but with its air perfumed by the products that lined its soaring shelves. Great products, great space. But what I loved most was that the owners were barely making ends meet because they had no skills in branding or business. A dream scenario for my agency! We had so much to offer and could really make a run at design awards and healthy profits. I was very excited. I outlined a plan to them for day-to-day operations, areas of responsibilities, visions, targets, and of course numbers. The process was fun and we soon struck a deal.

Did I mention that I was excited? I was very excited! More specifically, I was excited and non-present, because in my head I was already way down the road imagining the environmentally friendly, organic products we'd develop and the gorgeous new branding and packaging designs we'd create.

I also felt a sense of urgency. I was convinced that an opportunity like this wouldn't come around again. In my haste, I committed the No. 1 business blunder. I didn't read the room.

Had I read the room, I would have heard the former pop star say she didn't want to actually work much. She wanted to just glide in and out and be fabulous and social. Perform massages and facials? Not so much.

Had I read the room, I would have also picked up on the resentful vibe from the patchouli-and-granola co-owner who displayed open hostility toward anything business- or money-related, including yours truly.

The partnership commenced. Funds were transferred and design teams were rolled out.

It didn't take long for me to realize my mistake. Requests for basic things like staff and sales reports were ignored or fought because the owners didn't want to do boring paperwork. They just wanted to maintain the place's easygoing, drop-in-daycare vibe. Soon I learned that many spa clients were expressing disappointment at not getting their treatment from the person they'd booked. Former Pop Star was transferring many bookings to her partner.

Worst of all, I couldn't find a way to reach them either on the human level or the business level. I'm fluent in several languages, including New Age and business, but I was stumped, and frustration mounted on both sides. Eventually reports filtered back to me that Peace and Love had made derogatory comments about our agency to some of the spa clients.

It was time for a serious talk.

I met her in my office at the agency, a grownup place of business, in hopes that it would jolt her to cognition. It didn't, and the conversation soon turned surreal as she ranted about how humans are beyond saving because we'd rather poison our groundwaters with chemical-laden shampoos than give up our shiny, bouncy hair.

I had had enough. The deal had to end, and I wanted it to happen right then and there. I told her in no uncertain terms—and possibly some colorful language—what our immediate exit would entail.

As I waited for her to tell me whether they would repay our invested funds in return for our not suing for breach of contract, I looked at her. I mean really looked at her. That's when I realized she was pregnant. Early days, but definitely pregnant. I had just used a harsh tone with a pregnant woman. Sighing inwardly, I told her more gently to think it over, talk to her partner, and get back to me the next day.

When she left, I sank back in my chair and replayed all the pre-deal conversations in my head, matching each with a reason this deal had been doomed to fail. And I realized that this wasn't on the owners. It was on me. They had told me what to expect, through their words, energies, and actions. If only I had listened, paid attention, read the room."

Mind Skills

As we scan our own memories of times that we were completely out of touch, let's not get stuck in self-blame and woulda-coulda-shouldas. Frankly, at this point we're grateful for the many times we failed to pick up on obvious signals in business, especially early on, because we learn a lot from falling and even more from getting up.

We've fine-tuned our room-reading abilities over the years and credit it for many of our advancements and victories. Sure, it's great to be an industry expert and have a brilliant mind that can deliver, but if you're not reading the room it can all be for naught. Being insensitive or out of touch has killed more business deals than we can count.

In our individual quests to understand the intangible parameters of doing business, we've observed some important themes. Engineering caps on, coaching whistles in place? Let's explore room-reading and how to catch bullshit:

- Everything is energy

- Bullshit has its own frequency

- The ego is an unreliable room-reader

- An inner compass shows the way

Everything Is Energy

You know those CGI videos that zoom in on an object and dive through it into an even smaller reality over and over again? It's a great illustration of how life works. In the real world, we'd zoom in on matter and go into molecules, and then atoms, and then sub-atomic particles that aren't made of matter at all. Some of these particles don't even stick to one structure. They can change from a particle into a wave. The further we go, the more we realize that no matter how solid something seems, it's not made of anything. The zoomed-in truth is that everything is energy.

You can position yourself to recognize truths and possibilities by acknowledging that you are energy (your intentions, your emotions, your tone of voice, your body, your bank account) and that everything else is energy too (the conference table, the numbers on a spreadsheet, future possibilities, the other people in and beyond the room).

When you read the room to forecast outcomes, its energy is a signpost. It will tell you what you need to work on to make it happen—or if you should just pull the plug. In other words, before something becomes anything, it exists first in a pre-manifested energetic state that we don't yet perceive as a "thing." When you know everything is energy, you're able to read and interpret energy.

Bullshit Has Its Own Frequency

There may not be any studies about it, but we can all probably agree that bullshit has its own frequency. Our years in leadership, mentorship, and coaching roles have shown us that people who pay attention can detect bullshit. They know when they're being sold a bill of goods. They can spot a lie. They pick up on a room's energetic discord.

We're all energy that's part of a larger energy field, made up of the energy from everyone and everything. Through this energy connection, we can tell when people are not aligned within themselves. Something feels off. Their words don't match their body language, or their actions don't match the plan. In the worst case, we sense that their intentions are far removed from any acceptable value base. If we pay attention, we can feel it. It's bullshit.

A common business mistake is to focus on "the facts" and forget that even people who are completely out of self-alignment can muster their own "facts" but be unable to leverage their intuitive sense of misaligned energies. Those people follow the narrow, prescribed business path and make decisions from a limited perspective.

The human brain can process 11 million bits of information every second, but our conscious minds can handle only 40 to 50 bits of information per second. That's a whopping difference in processing capabilities, and our conscious mind, our logic and reasoning brain, simply can't process fast enough to detect the bullshit frequencies.

Cleaning up our subconscious minds and listening to messages from a deeper, more abstract part of ourselves is the ticket to a well-functioning bullshit radar.

Take an inventory of times when your so-called business sense overrode your bullshit radar. How did it register? What did it feel like? Were there any other signals? Start paying attention to this as you move forward in business. Trust your own system to pick up on the distinct wavelength of bullshit. And the next time your radar goes off, believe it.

Mr. Ego Can't Read a Room

Business will always have a degree of ego attached to it, but when your primary drive and intentions are ego-based, it's harder to read situations. The ego wants to compete, compare, and argue. It wants the most attention, the most praise, the most money, the best seat. It wants to get and take as much as possible as fast as possible. It prefers to have the last word in any matter.

Linda's ego was already winning design awards and raking in the cash. No wonder she couldn't read the room. She couldn't even hear the meanings of words over the noise of her own hubris and limited mindset.

Winning is one of life's paradoxes. When you push full-on for what you want, your chances of getting it go down. Force creates counterforce that will exhaust you. Instead, suspend your immediate need for attention, gain, or gratification. It's okay to let go of your ego for a bit. You won't make bad decisions. In fact, quite the opposite. Picking up on signals beyond your critical mind requires a level of inner silence that simply can't *be* when the ego is whirring. When we suspend our personal agendas and connect our energy to other energies, the unified field of unlimited potential opens. That's when you can make good decisions.

An Inner Compass Shows the Way

Clarity about our own values and the ability to operate with non-judging, present-moment awareness aid greatly in reading a room. Even if we don't feel able to tune in to the energy, if we establish confluency between our own values and priorities, and our thoughts, words, emotions, and actions, it's easier to notice when someone or something is not aligning with you. Make a habit of noticing the baseline of people's energy. Before long, you'll be able to pick up on the misalignments within others.

A Maturing Radar

When people who are in self-alignment become practiced at room reading, it brings successes that lead us to trust ourselves more. Understanding our own priorities and purpose makes life decisions and doing business much easier. We simply follow our curiosity and joy, asking *What is mine to do?* If it doesn't feel natural or good to you, it's just not for you.

We don't mean that the right choice is always going to be the easy one. Far from it. The thing that feels right may require us to work hard, get dirty, push limits. But inconvenience and suffering aren't tick marks on some moral measuring stick. That's old thinking. When we understand what is ours to do, we'll choose to pass on other things. *Not my battle. Not my fight. Not my calling.*

A mature radar lets you trust your inner prompts. If someone pops into your head in a certain way, it's a sign that you should reach out to them. If you feel inclined to take a different route home, take it. If you're in a conversation and an insistent thought is clamoring in your head, speak it aloud.

Linda: "As an executive coach, I've learned to bring up what my inner prompt shows me. It may be such a small thing that my mind wants to dismiss it. I once said to a job-seeking coaching client, "I keep seeing a bright blue dress, so I thought I'd mention it." She didn't look at me sideways or tell me I was nuts. She exclaimed, "I can't believe you said that! I've been agonizing over what to wear to my final interview. My instinct was to wear my blue dress, but I thought I should go with basic black or power red. That was really helpful! Thank you." When these seemingly small things turn out to be correct and helpful, it trains us for accuracy on bigger things.

Speaking of bigger things, these flashes can have much larger implications, so it's important to do this tactfully and ethically. I once told a coaching client, "As I'm tuning in to you, I feel a pain near my heart, so I'm mentioning it. Don't be alarmed, but consider getting it checked out." These are prompts, not facts, and it's important to present them that way. Coincidentally, she had a doctor's appointment scheduled for the next day, and because of what I said, she asked that her heart be checked. The tests uncovered a condition that required medication.

When I trust these inner promptings, they usually turn out to be helpful. And please know that I am not a witch, a psychic, or a guru. I've just learned to tune in. It's a surrendering of ego and a conscious release of agenda. It's a platform created by continual practice at keeping my mind as calm and clean as possible. If this bouncy little tomboy can do it, so can you."

Stephanie: *"As an electrical engineer, the concept of reading rooms is familiar to me. It's a matter of recognizing and fine-tuning the inputs and outputs. When I started out in engineering, punch cards were used to deliver commands to computers. Punch cards! Cards with holes in them! The computer made calculations based on where the holes were. I'm not a hundred years old—that's just what there was. Then things advanced and we moved into the keyboard age. The new means of input led to more sophisticated outputs. A lot has happened since then too, of course. We've added everything from the mouse to biological touch screens, gone from wired to wireless, and now enjoy audio and video outputs that have much greater clarity and sophistication.*

As electromagnetic beings ourselves, we can develop our input sensitivity to create more sophisticated outputs. Better mind skills training improves our ability to filter out interfering frequencies. What we do allow through will resonate with who we are and why we're here."

Reading rooms is a powerful tool that should be used only with good intentions. Fortunately, it only really works when you do it from the heart.

As you practice your skills—with a big dose of self-love and humor—our hope is that you will have fewer moments of looking back in regret and will instead look forward with curiosity, brilliance, and a sense of service. You are the leader the world is hoping for.

--

"Although the human mind likes to believe that it is 'of course' dedicated to truth, in reality, what it really seeks is confirmation of what it already believes. The ego is innately prideful and does not welcome the revelation that much of its beliefs are merely perceptual illusions."

~ David Hawkins

--

Nine
Future Orchestrator

As leaders, we all want a say in the way we shape the future. With all things moving faster and faster, leaders today are trying to find something that might make the chaotic present more manageable and allow some kind of control over future returns: A system, a belief, a process.

As discussed in Chapter Four on executive confidence, we don't believe time management is the answer. We understand the inclination: Things move fast, and everyone must get more done in less time. But let's forget about time for a moment and think about energy.

We have discovered that managing *energy*—our own and our teams'—yields much better results than managing time. It's really about *orchestrating* energy, which is done in the present moment. Stay with us here because the intricacies around energy orchestration are fascinating. We're going deep!

When you want to impact events and influence people, you need to be connected to the larger field of energy that makes events happen and gets people to light up and engage. Need a metaphor? Think of a river. (All metaphors fail at some point, but this will do for our purposes now). When we visualize the river of Life, we see a natural but contained flow of events. We may also spy obstacles that interrupt and shape the river's flow, like sharp rocks or floating debris. Like life events, some will collide and force adjustments in the flow. Others will float by rapidly but still influence everything around them. Time is a factor in the river's progress, but what really matters is the flow.

In the river of your own life, currents pull at you—bad breaks, conflict, loss—that feel outside your control and drain your energy. These life events can never be controlled completely, and that's okay. We're humans, here for a human experience, and a little tumult and trouble here and there can sometimes get things moving. The sooner we accept that turbulent waters are just part of the flow of life, the sooner we'll find a better flow.

A big obstacle to creating good and abundant flow can be found in our collective programming. Our instinct is to navigate the river of Life by swimming upriver, fighting against the current to reach some prize. Bosses and owners have always prospered from others' hard work, so they long ago decreed that working hard is the name of the game. We have been programmed to believe that the only way to get ahead in life is to work yourself to death and if you don't you're not worthy of good returns.

If an heiress sails by on her magnificent yacht, it's easy to become resentful. *She didn't earn that!* But if we were to learn that it was a non-heiress who has worked 80-hour weeks for decades and sacrificed to afford that boat, we'd be totally okay with that. *Good for her!*

Many judge themselves this way. *If I don't work hard, I don't deserve good things.* When we jump into the river of Life, we instinctively start swimming upstream. *We must battle! No pain, no gain! The tough get going!* Year after year, we keep working hard and putting in our time, always swimming against the current without ever stopping to reflect on how things really work in the river of Life.

What if you wanted to have downstream journeys? Not going backward, but flowing in alignment with everything life brings? What if you could flow effortlessly, awake to connections, opportunities, and solutions? As you learn to flow with life, you get so good at listening and sensing the flow that soon you'll know what's coming around the next bend.

All we're asking you to do right now is to take a closer look at the concept of working yourself to death for success. Then we can start learning how to orchestrate the future.

Linda: *"I was living in Los Angeles, working as a creative director at a strategic agency whose clients were huge multinational corporations with large-scale development projects and complicated communication needs. I could easily have worked eighty hours a week, and sometimes I did. If I hadn't had some wonderful friends in the entertainment industry who frequently cajoled me into being their plus-one for parties and premieres, I'd probably have worked even more. I was just on the cusp of waking up to the importance of work-life-balance.*

I'm Swedish, remember, and as a foreigner living in the United States it's crucial that I keep up with the paperwork to retain my permanent residency status. Before moving to Los Angeles, I had lived in New York City, where the enforcing agency was INS (Immigration and Naturalization Services). My "green card," a stamp in my passport, was coming up for renewal, but because I was still registered in New York, I would have to travel for it. The timing of various projects made me postpone the trip until the very last minute. I booked my flight to arrive in NYC on the morning of the expiration date.

If you've ever taken the redeye from LAX to JFK, you know that you arrive in New York City ridiculously early in the morning. Even after the ride into Manhattan, you still have to wait for the city to come to life. I planned to visit a favorite peaceful spot before the morning rush swirled around it. I wanted to shoot some photos in the day's first light and get in a much-needed meditation.

The date loomed. I knew I needed to pack at least a small bag for the quick trip, but I just didn't feel like doing it. Weird. When I told some coworkers I really didn't want to go, their reactions ranged all the way from "Are you crazy?" to "Have you lost your mind?"

I knew they were right, but I still didn't want to go! While my logical brain understood that I would be risking my permanent resident status, that I could lose my job, my apartment, and get kicked out of the U.S., another part of me was very clear: "That may be true, but I'm still not going."

My flight date arrived and I didn't get on the plane. My friends and coworkers were horrified. One in particular, a fellow Swede living in L.A., knew the risk of my choice and was furious. So much so, she told me later, that she had considered putting our friendship on an indefinite pause.

It was she who called me early the next morning, rattled and perplexed, to deliver tragic news. The expiration date on the stamp in my passport was September 11, 2001. My favorite place to visit was Austin J. Tobin Plaza at the World Trade Center. I would have been at the foot of the Twin Towers when disaster struck.

In the end, the INS give dispensations to those whose status had been impacted by the horrific events and aftermath of 9/11, and I embarked on some profound soul-searching. I wanted to understand how I'd come to have my premonition. How was it even possible?"

Mind Skills

Throughout this book, we've asked you to open your mind a little further, open your heart a little wider, and let go of old ideas about how things work and what your limitations are. We're glad you've chosen to come along. Not because you think we have all the answers, or because you think there might be something wrong with you. We don't, and there isn't. We're here to give you the benefit of our hard-won experience and help you explore possibilities for making conscious impact in business. Every leader can play large roles or small but important parts.

Allowing the Flow

Your ego may protest, but for just a moment, suspend your beliefs about how "working hard" is the key to success and picture your river of Life. Is it one you can easily slip into, read, predict, navigate, and lay back? Is there the power of movement and flow to support you? Can you rest easy in the belief that everything you really want awaits downstream?

"Work hard" mottoes like "*Genius is one percent inspiration and 99 percent perspiration*" are etched into our subconscious programming. That famous quote is attributed to Thomas Edison, inventor of the lightbulb, phonograph, motion pictures, and more. But as is the case with many vintage quotes from famous men, maybe it shouldn't be. In the early 1890s, American academic Kate Sanborn described genius as a mix of inspiration (talent and creativity) and perspiration (effort). When told of Ms. Sanborn's original statement, Edison agreed with it and said he would quantify the breakdown as 2% inspiration, 98% perspiration. (This anecdote is extra fun now that a light-bulb emoji is used to signify an inspired idea.)

Human consciousness has evolved so much in the ensuing decades. The requirements of the mechanical and industrial age differ vastly from those of our age of post-information, digital transformation, and artificial intelligence. If your goal is to make it to the big leagues, let go of history and make way for your destiny. You can do it now.

When we release old ways of thinking about work, we're freed to impact the future rather than dwell on the past.

As you examine your thinking about flow, it may seem that most people float idly down a stream. Lazy sheep, right? If you push yourself harder than anyone else, you'll deserve and win a spot at the top. But that's not how it works.

First: Many people think they have tough lives. Most think they're working hard all the time. Everybody is exhausted! But ask a hugely successful person about their day. Most don't work harder than other people. They're not exhausted all the time. They make time for wellness, travel, and fun.

They work smarter. They're in a different flow.

Second: There is no prize at the top of the stream. Being the hardest worker does not guarantee success. Ask anyone who has three jobs but barely makes ends meet. The prize is the ability to flow with less effort, see connections that others don't, meet people with joy and curiosity, jump on opportunities when they arise, and make interesting things happen. Battling the current will only exhaust you.

Play-by Play

"Orchestrating the future" is an abstract area of leadership that we can call "intuition." A deeper knowing, an inspired state. Business shies away from such words, demanding facts and figures and quantifiable results. But great visionaries in the big leagues don't play by those limited rules. They're tapped into something bigger, a universal intelligence of great ideas and a sense of the future. And before you write yourself off as not being a genius or having access to an intelligence superfield, stop. You *are* universal intelligence. You *are* genius. In fact, you are evolution unfolding. Higher levels of consciousness are constantly at your fingertips.

In a world that demands academic research and scientific proof, standard approaches and metrics are confounded by consciousness and human superpowers. Science, logic, psychology, and Western philosophy struggle to study these concepts, but we can gain insights from leading-edge experts like physicist Nassim Haramein, founder of the Resonance Science Foundation. We can find inspiration in the cosmological roadmap of Jude Currivan, the fascinating conversations between Nobel laureates Albert Einstein and Indian poet Rabindranath Tagore, or the discussion of the cosmic self that has emerged between Deepak Chopra and physicist Menas Kafatos.

We're not here to lecture about plasma, quantum mechanics, the chemical composition of reality, or spirituality versus science. We invite you to lean into your own curiosity about life's conundrums. Connect the dots and see what resonates. On the road to accessing higher levels of consciousness, we are asking you to be okay with the unknown.

If you go where few leaders dare, you'll be in largely unknown territory. Mind skills will help you navigate.

The time has finally come to explore mind training that goes beyond your own mind and beyond time to intuit the future, catch sparks of inspiration, tune into high creativity, befriend your evolutionary impulses, and make all of it practical and real. Sufi mystic poet Jalaluddin Rumi famously described this playing field:

Out beyond ideas of wrongdoing and rightdoing,
There is a field. I'll meet you there.
When the soul lies down in that grass,
The world is too full to talk about.
Ideas, language, even the phrase each other
Doesn't make any sense.

These beautiful words are step-by-step instructions for connecting with a higher level of consciousness.

When we study universal intelligence and feel future stirrings, we enter a space that's beyond judgment and measuring. That's where we'll meet now – not as individuals whose professional title represents their primary identity, but as souls, something even bigger than the "self."

The instruction goes on to remind us to be fully connected to the earth with our minds open to the universe. No need for our limited words or the notion that we are separate from each other. The universal evolutionary intelligence that directs the river of Life is beyond what makes sense in our Newtonian world. Evolutionary intelligence creates manifestations, because it not only sees what's coming but in fact lined things up to make it happen. And it has a much bigger picture of what is yet to come.

As an impactful leader in the big leagues, you need to be fully immersed in the intelligence that creates this world.

Future Stirrings

As we dive deeper into the subject of orchestrating the future, consider the possibility that you already *are* the future. In the river analogy, the flowing water affects and changes everything it touches, shaping the future.

What you do impacts what the river becomes. That's why letting go is so important. If you cling to the shoreline of your own river instead of changing your ways or opening up for greater possibilities and higher levels of consciousness, you can't flow down to where you can have impact. Instead, you'll get hit by whatever people decide to throw into the river while you're holding on for dear life.

Once you've let go, your actions and movements impact the water, and you tune into everything else that is impacting the flow. Trust the evolutionary impulses and know they are connected to events and qualities that are ready to emerge into the world. That's how we sometimes "just know" things. We just know we should wait. We just know we shouldn't work with that person. We just know we should choose a different route. "Just knowing" is fundamentally different from the knowing of the ego that believes it has all the answers. "Just knowing" is not personal. It's not attached to image or prestige.

Being connected to a flow of consciousness is also why we sometimes have a specific sense that something is about to happen. Intuition will tell us that something is a good idea or a very bad idea. *This will flop,* or *That is the only safe option,* or *This unexpected thing is exactly what we should be focusing on right now.* So-called "logical people" may try to talk us down, but this sense is bigger than logic. It's connected to an evolutionary arc that brings a calm type of certainty.

Both of us have been in this place of "just knowing." We've been doubted or had our results dismissed as luck. Connected people, though, recognize that our knowing is not about personal truths but a larger collective intelligence that feels as natural to them as it does to us.

The battle has two fronts:

1. The internal struggle to restrain the selfish ego from severing our connection to the knowing.

2. The external mission to gain the confidence of others to trust in the knowing.

The latter becomes easier when you have a good track record.

We want to make sense of it. How does it work? We're not psychics or fortune tellers. Sometimes we even hesitate to label these feelings as intuition. Our theory of the phenomenon ties back to the river analogy. Life is a river of energy from which we absorb "just knowing."

Think about it. When water rushes down a river and hits a big rock, it can't go through it. Meeting the rock is a big event that interrupts the water's flow, initially forcing it to ripple back before it resurges and finds its way around the rock. That's how we visualize these premonitions. If we are sensitive to the river's flow, we will recognize even the slightest change in speed or direction, feeling the ripple before we reach the rock. It may present abstractly as a feeling of a general yes or no, or it may be a flash of specific information: *Choose this, not that. Sell at 35. Vacation in Bali.* Be the water and not the rock.

This is a good time to remind yourself that connection doesn't function properly when the ego is in charge. Ego means separation and disconnection. It's when the ego is suspended that these connections become much clearer. Without the ego's agenda bigfooting our behavior, we are more open to the agenda of evolutionary benefit—including the best innovations, solutions, and plans to serve humanity.

History shows that "business sense" is rooted in evolutionary impulses.

We're all tiny but key parts of a greater evolutionary intelligence. We each contribute to it when we acknowledge and examine our feelings and impulses. So many managers and leaders have ideas and visions but don't follow through on them. It's like saying "*I sense there will be this type of event further down the river*" but not planning a response, gathering resources, or taking action.

A leader who doesn't have a clear mind and a goal with a plan to achieve it may fall back on activity, but activity does not equate to movement. Without consciousness and connection, it can be more like rearranging deck chairs on the Titanic. People go to meetings, share beautiful PowerPoints, and talk about the same old topics in different ways. It usually doesn't solve a problem any more than a new chair arrangement would have prevented the Titanic disaster.

An orchestrator creates their future before they engage. Write down your ultimate objective and outline your plan to achieve it. Include possible obstacles and how you'll address them. You want movement, not activity.

Stephanie: *"Being the one who sees the future can be lonely. It's on us to try to convince the people standing by the river to jump into freezing cold water full of sharp rocks by telling them, "Don't worry! It gets better further downstream!" But if you feel strongly about the path you've seen, your energy will bring them along too.*

Early in my cable career, I put forward a new product idea that I knew would be a game changer. My plate was already full and no one around me thought the idea was worth my time. But I just knew.

I kept fostering the project, quietly moving it along without impacting other, more visible programs. Eventually, I convinced senior leaders to let me sign a trial agreement with an unknown vendor and we all started to talk about the new business opportunity and its potential revenue. It took years to prove and the process was strewn with technical and business challenges. But I knew something big was going to happen, and it did. My side-of-the-desk project grew into a new type of television advertising, a targeted, addressable model that's still used now, 20 years later. A healthy new business was created."

River Protection

An appealing thing about the concept of life as a river is that it's *your* river. Even though we often have to swim among others' limitations and irritations, they're like the rocks in the river. The right mind skills can guide you around them and keep you in your flow. After all, it's not their river.

What you allow in your river is up to you. More precisely, what you perceive that other people will add to your river is what ends up in your river. The choice is yours. This book is about cleaning up our metaphorical rivers so we can perceive and interpret the world from a healed subconscious mind, forgiving heart, and generous spirit. Mind, heart, and energy skills let us co-create the reality we want to live in.

Your river is connected to everything and everyone else while also being your own unique experience.

You are a spiritual being who is having a human experience. Everyone's river is dictated by evolutionary wishes that manifest in ways humans may never grasp. But while you can't control everything and everyone, you can choose what meanings you impart to objects and events in your river. You can control your relationship with the river, adjust your attitude about it, decide what to learn from it, and choose a path forward.

As you already know, people may throw rocks at you, push you underwater, or dump toxic waste into your river. Your new River Protection Agency can handle it. Acknowledge that these things are happening in a mind you created. See them for what they are and then those people can no longer despoil your river.

Stephanie: *"I've often heard Linda say, "Water what you want to grow." In other words, give your attention to the things you want to nurture. I believe our thoughts manifest the future, and that maxim is a helpful reminder to focus on the things that are important to me. I've worked in my own meditation practice to train my mind away from thoughts that don't benefit me. It's challenging under any circumstances, and perhaps even more so in the business world with its annoying, frustrating interactions and incidents. Be mindful of your thoughts and words because they will manifest.*

For example, everyone loves to bash the arrogant manager. We all feel great after we shoot out some choice words about the boss who disrespected us or made us do something we disagreed with. I'll cut right to the chase: Don't. The bad energy of those thoughts, words, and emotions will manifest and make things worse. I've seen it countless times in the corporate world.

Early in my career in technology, I'd spend weeks or months working through the details of a technical strategy or development plan only to have people at more removed levels push for changes to the plan or even to the technical solution itself. People who work in tech know that engineers and scientists typically have an attitude of "I know better and I'm always right." Reader, I was one of those people. I would become so frustrated at being questioned or challenged by people I didn't think were experts. This frustration would morph into anger and bring friction to interactions. Over the years, I honed my ability to recognize this pattern. Much of my career success can be attributed to replacing negative thoughts with positive energy.

In practical terms, this often means pausing to listen to feedback. When people are finished critiquing, I offer information and insights to help them see a solution, agree on it, and move forward. I don't allow negative thoughts to take hold in my mind, much less get anywhere near my mouth. I replace them with constructive thoughts about the person or situation I instinctively wanted to trash.

I don't mean you should bite your tongue, swallow your anger, and never speak up. I'm saying you can alchemize your anger into resolve. Be clear-eyed about finding and using your positive energy. You can bet that as a woman in tech, I've had extremely rude and even derogatory things said right to my face. I have been mistaken as the coffee girl or a marketing assistant in rooms where I am the expert on the subject matter. I have had people sabotage me. I've been advised in no uncertain terms that I don't belong. Many of my executive friends and colleagues have said, "I don't know how you do it," especially when I continue to work with and be cordial to people whom they think have done me wrong. I do it by finding and exercising my positive energy. It's always there to draw on in moments of frustration. I never feel like a pushover or that I'm letting people walk over me. I don't allow my inner self to be rattled by their arrogance. If I did that, I couldn't orchestrate the future I want to have."

The Floodgate Paradox

There are both *systemic* and *individual* instigators of frustration, resentment, and hopelessness. Although both need to be addressed, your entry point will always be through the individual. As you work to orchestrate your river, there's a paradox to acknowledge before you can make bigger changes happen. Call it the Yes-No paradox. Before you can say yes to life, you must also be able to say no.

The big life is an interconnected life that can make your river flow in a beautiful and meaningful way. The small life is an ego-driven life with no ability to make things flow.

Business egos say a big yes to a small life. Yes to promotions, higher salaries, bigger offices, private jets. Growing means making more money, buying more companies, taking over more categories.

But eventually, another voice emerges. It says no. Those yeses didn't bring fulfillment, meaning, or joy. Ego always says "Yes! I want more!" But when No finds its voice, decisions are made differently. *No, I am not interested in that lateral promotion. No, you can't buy me off with a bigger office. No, I am not willing to support a system that does not align with my values. I sense something different coming my way.*

Only then can we say yes to the big life.

Then we have the capacity to expand with the evolution of human consciousness, growing both on an individual level and as part of the cosmic expansion, doing the inner work that's necessary to cultivate growth. We don't let our egos dictate our decisions. We flow in a much-expanded river with endless opportunities for connections, solutions, innovation, and co-creation. We find deeply meaningful ways to use the gifts we find in the vastness of Self. That's the new yes.

Yes – No – Yes.

Like a long, winding river, the new yes naturally finds itself in a life so big, powerful, and intentional that systemic shifts can happen. We all want to fight injustices and change systems of power abuse. Expanding our own rivers may be the best route. Having conscious people in positions of power at scale will bring real changes to systems around the world.

Meanwhile, don't hamper yourself with a need to control time or people. The river of energy that surrounds us, that *is* us, is a lot more fun to play with. When we make the mind shift to orchestrating energy instead of managing people and time, we prime our minds to shape the flow of the future. So conduct your own river. Choose what you want to allow in it. Above all, don't forget that we're supposed to have fun while we create music that encourages harmony between people, events, perceived realities, and time.

--

No matter what happens in space, space can never be harmed or destroyed. Likewise, no matter what arises in the mind, no matter how violent or deluded it is, the nature of mind has always and will always be pure.

~ Chamtrul Rinpoche

--

Ten
Helping the Team Win

If a speaker stands before an English-speaking audience and asks, "WHAT MAKES IT WORK?" the audience will shout back "TEAMWORK!"

Teamwork is inherent to our human existence. Prehistoric societies wouldn't have survived without members working together to find food and shelter and fend off predators. In the present day, whether we're playing a game, staging a play, building a house, or fighting a war, teamwork greatly increases the chances of success. It's part of our deepest programming. Why, then, does this ancient programming fall away in a business setting?

On a soccer team, some positions are meant to direct the play, others to score goals, and another, the goalkeeper, to prevent the other team from scoring. But sometimes a striker saves the ball on the goal line. Sometimes the goalkeeper scores a goal. Players are on the field to help the team win. There's no room for "that's not my job."

Today's business culture isn't conducive to teamwork. Most environments still focus on individual performance in determining compensation and advancement. To have impact in the big leagues, we have to understand what it means to be a team, to be interconnected.

A leader's key responsibility is helping team members grow into team *players*. Even the ones who've never thought about it, let alone been trained for it. Like soccer coaches, leaders are supposed to train their players to help the team win.

Stephanie: *"In the early 2010s I was asked to lead a major project to create a product that would store recorded video in the cloud. Now the digital video recorder, or DVR, is such a common technology it's easy to forget how recent it is. It didn't exist until a team of engineers and project folks made it happen!*

For those unfamiliar with cloud technologies, here's a quick primer: Content and applications live on servers in distributed locations. Our devices connect to those servers via networks and the internet.

At the time, this kind of technology was just being developed. The initial idea came from a very forward-thinking executive team with a vision of giving customers a superior experience by removing the constraints of local storage. Instead of content being recorded on a disc drive in set-top boxes, the content would upload to a remote facility for ingest and storage. This product is called RS-DVR: remote storage digital video recorder.

Successful execution would push the whole industry ahead. Other cable providers could add the same features to their products. I remember the technical leadership team scribbling out notes and talking excitedly about the development and engineering needed to make it work. My role would oversee software and infrastructure. My team would make the video feeds, storage, encoders, playback systems, and networking function in this new architecture. It was exciting stuff, and I was glad to be part of it.

There were many other teams, each headed by other senior technology leaders. The IT teams had to figure out how to bill and manage the new product. The UI teams had to create an interface on a set-top box that could connect to and control the cloud systems. Before I bore you with too much detail (too late?), the gist is that a ton of technical coordination was needed in order to make it all work. Plus, we wanted to be the first to do it!

As with most complex projects, it soon became clear that these various missions had to be coordinated across the teams. The program management office was run by a woman I can only describe as kickass. She called it like it was and exuded power with every move. She had grown frustrated with all the parallel reporting across the teams and wanted to name a cross-team executive leader.

When she announced this in a large meeting, everyone eyed the team leaders and waited to see who'd volunteer. No one did. Perhaps they were concerned that it would be too much work in addition to leading their own teams. Perhaps they were put off by the fact that no one knew if the product would work or ever be deployed.

I raised my hand. I knew it was either a really stupid move or a career-defining opportunity. Either way, I was signing up for another huge workload.

My new cross-function required me to work closely with the other teams. As the project evolved, it became evident that moving the recording process into the cloud was more than a technical project. Content handling meant legal and operational considerations. It was determined that a tech team leader would have to work with the legal and product teams to ensure system compliance. I was known for being able to explain technology in simple language and had experience with being deposed and testifying.

I worked with our legal team, explaining how the new system would work and answering their questions while my team continued to work on the end-to-end product. Now I held three tough roles, and I wrestled with the idea that I should hold only as much power as I could be accountable for. But I couldn't backpedal. We were committed to the program and close to holding the product trials.

I'd already made a number of "save the day" contributions to this big, *complex, groundbreaking project. Now I had to open up my thinking. I realized things would move forward faster if more people had decision-making authority.*

A very talented engineer who worked for me was leading the video and system engineering work. He wasn't yet a vice president, but he was talented and engaged. Knowing it wouldn't absolve me of ultimate responsibility, I passed one of my torches to him. He would represent me at most of the technical meetings, and I empowered him to make decisions and set plans with partners and vendors. It was a huge personal relief to relinquish some work while still feeling responsible and supportive. It gave me the headspace I needed to work on the bigger-picture items.

This memory stands out because it was when I realized that sharing power can be more effective than delegating it. It opened the floodgates of progress on this project. Things flowed along nicely...and then I learned still another lesson about the tough area between giving up some control and still being responsible for outcomes.

The executives and teams held a scrum meeting every week or so to conduct technical reviews and share project updates. We'd go down a screen-projected list of discussion items and talk about statuses and desired outcomes and things that needed attention or support. Items of special concern would appear in red.

In one of these meetings, one of my team's assignments blazed red on the screen to indicate 'At risk for at least two weeks with no anticipated completion date.' After some probing, we found that it was related to a problem with one vendor's equipment. The device was part of the chain of systems that worked on the video stream as it was being ingested, conditioning it for playback. But there was no playback. No video. No solution. Shoot. I had to get this fixed.

I scrambled for time to spend with my team while they tried to solve the problem. All the other teams were moving along except the ones whose work was blocked by my team's issue, and I felt terrible about that. My team and I sat through the next few scrum meetings feeling like failures, our item still onscreen in red. Every week the Program

Manager unleashed a barrage of questions. "Is there an update here?" "When will the solution be ready?" "Do you know how many other items are depending on this resolution?" The program was slipping further behind every day. It was miserable. I admit also feeling frustrated that even though I had passed control of the team to someone else, I was still the one who had to take the heat at every meeting. It's hard to share power and still be accountable.

After a few weeks of this torture, the PM demanded to know why the problem hadn't yet been solved. I wanted to scream, "If I knew how to solve it, it would be solved by now!"

Good engineering training teaches you that there are no unsolvable problems. Only ones whose solutions haven't yet presented themselves. A few weeks later, with guidance from my senior engineer, the team finally identified the issue. It wasn't terribly sexy, just a configuration mistake deep in one of the servers. The team cleaned up the configuration files and I finally had success to report and satisfactory answers to give. We were so excited that we practically danced our way to the next status meeting. But wouldn't you know it, for the first time over the course of the project, neither the executives nor the PM were present. What the what? My anticipated moment of triumph was lost. A stand-in for the project leader went down the list: Software, check. Architecture, check. IT, check. Video, check. "Looks like we're in good shape." Well, that was anticlimactic. No cheers, no applause. Just "Okay, see you next week."

But celebrations did come out of it. One was immediate and inside me: I felt even more connected to my teams and so happy that I hadn't let the difficulties diminish that connection. When things go wrong it's tempting to blame others or let your disappointment and anger show. This experience taught me that a leader should find ways to lower the team's stress levels so they can do their best work.

The second celebration came when the project group went on to win a technical Emmy Award for deploying what is now known as RS-DVR. I still use this product in my home today, and you probably do too."

Mind Skills

We don't have to sell you on teamwork. You know how key it is. It's just so hard to achieve in business. Why? Simple. Because human nature works against it in competitive business structures.

Let's explore the relevant research and our own observations about how to create strong teams. We'll talk about trust, collaboration, conflict, and, yes, how to deal with difficult people.

Trust

Trust is foundational to creating a successful team environment. Team members have to be able to trust their leaders and each other to be competent, accountable, and when necessary, flexible. The best employees score highly not only on performance-related metrics but also on trustworthiness. Lack of trust tanks more situations than performance issues do.

But how do we trust each other?

In a recent study on trust in the workplace, 87,000 leaders participated in the Zenger/Folkman Extraordinary Leader 360 Assessment. A score in the 80th percentile or above indicates a potential leader. But those who scored in or above the 60th percentile in three key areas were shown to outperform, meaning that those who rate just slightly above average in these areas will receive much more trust from their team. The three elements are:

1. **Positive Relationships**. Trustworthy leaders generate cooperation and better conflict resolution. They are in touch with team members' issues and concerns and balance a drive for results with caring for teammates and colleagues. They give honest feedback in a helpful way.

2. **Good Judgment/Expertise**. Trustworthy leaders are well-informed and knowledgeable. They display good judgment when making decisions. They anticipate and respond quickly to problems. These qualities make others trust their ideas and opinions.

3. **Consistency**. Trustworthy leaders walk the talk. They are role models who set good examples. They honor commitments, keep promises, and will go above and beyond to do it.

What struck us as most noteworthy is that a poor score in just one of these three areas sinks that person's trust score. Scoring above average on Good Judgment and Consistency but not on Positive Relationships will result in a below-average trust score.

Another fascinating finding is that Positive Relationships is the most important of the three. It makes sense. Without trust it's impossible to build a winning team, but we don't trust each other if we don't have positive relationships. Expertise and consistency are important, but they won't put you over the top without your also having the respect that comes from positive relationships.

Trust is a deep mind and heart skill that's crucial for both business and personal life. We can acknowledge that evil takes place but trust that ultimately the world is good. We know there are people who behave selfishly or cruelly, but we trust that most people are good. We're not telling you to bury your head in the sand. We're saying that this imperfect world is filled with tremendous beauty and many joyous possibilities. Life in the big leagues requires us to see trying times as character-building, setbacks as valuable lessons, and personal disappointments as opportunities to experience humanity. We can show up and trust that we'll figure things out together.

Collaboration

Good collaboration is the basis of a winning team. The word "collaboration" comes from the Latin "collaborare" which means "working together." Uniting to achieve a common goal is engaging and inspiring. The word gained a negative connotation after World War II that may have seeped into our subconscious minds: "Traitorous cooperation with an occupying enemy."

Those definitions seem diametrically opposed: We strive to work together but may be in cahoots with the enemy. *Will they steal my ideas? Are they vying for my position? Who is going to take credit for the work of the team—or worse, for my own contributions?*

An obstacle to collaboration can be found in the often misunderstood concept of "survival of the fittest." Originally coined in the 1860s by English philosopher Herbert Spencer and made famous by Charles Darwin, it's taken to mean that nature winnows out those too weak to survive. Along these lines, the business world fostered a tough environment of competition in which showing weakness is anathema. But in 2015, something mind-blowing was observed.

Here's what Dr. Kurt Johnson, an evolutionary biologist and interfaith scholar, said in 2020 on a Becoming of Business broadcast:

> "*We were told from the time of Darwin that evolution was survival of the fittest. It was all about competition, about who comes out on top. That created the shark-tank environment called Social Darwinism – the best competitor wins. This came to dominate politics and business in the 19th and 20th centuries, because we assumed that's what nature does.*
>
> "*But when we looked at nature, we thought, 'That's kind of weird,' because nature is always in balance. As of 2015, the mainstream scientific establishment, based on all the new data it could look at with current technology, came to realize that that idea of Darwinian evolution was wrong. It wasn't that the "survival of the fittest" was wrong, but the definition changes as you go to levels of complexity – and particularly with a conscious species that needs to make conscious choices.*
>
> ***What is now called the Knowledge of Group Selection and Hierarchical Selection—how groups make decisions—holds that groups always select what is best for the whole. They select the group's highest purpose.***
>
> *Dr. Johnson continues: "This is a complete sea-change in evolutionary biology. It's redefining natural selection and also redefining sociobiology, which is the whole field of science of how organisms in society work. So, the truth now is that nature selects from cooperation. Fitness is the best cooperator in*

any level of complexity or conscious being. Here's where this goes: It creates a situation where nature can't make these choices if we don't offer them up as possibilities. In a natural process, that's called mutation. If the mutation has an advantage, it chooses it. That's how the biological process works in natural selection. But "conscious selection" requires both the head and the heart, and it requires human beings to make choices.

Evolution wants to choose the thing that's best for the whole group, but it can't do it if we don't put out the behaviors and models that offer those clear choices.

Science can look at data and turn on a dime, and science changed its mind in 2015. It's a very difficult adjustment for business, economics, and politics to make after 150 years of Darwinian theory. Can we adapt to a new culture that's based on the way evolution really works?"

When collaborating seems hard, it's because we're erroneously programmed to think we're working against each other. Company systems perpetuate this zero-sum thinking. We've got to overcome the false notions that we can't all be winners and that the "weak" must be winnowed out. Instead, we should build systems of incentives and advancement paths that honor the evolutionary truth: Those who collaborate, succeed.

We're in a better position to break into the big leagues when we understand that good team decisions are based on the group's highest purpose.

Conflict

A team divided is a team defeated. If we don't address our ingrained resistance to collaboration and pull back on our persistent Me-focus, we will go on creating breeding grounds for conflict.

While it's hard to quantify the impact that conflict has on a business's bottom line, we believe conflict steals energy, stifles innovative processes, and stands in the way of team flow and quality work product.

Some view conflict as negative and detrimental. Others think it produces motion and growth. Is there such a thing as healthy conflict? It usually doesn't *feel* healthy.

There are two types of conflict:

1. Task-related disagreements

2. Personal disagreements

The differences are monumental.

Task-related disagreements are related to the work at hand. What's the best solution, what should be prioritized, who should be responsible for what, etc.

Personal disagreements are very different. Typically, they're about resentment or disrespect toward someone else's character, personality, or life choices. These conflicts can present as task-related but actually stem from personal judgments and disagreements. Often word choices are a giveaway: Accusatory (you, you're, my), judgmental (ridiculous, stupid, sucks), demonizing (always, never). Even a belittling or condescending tone speaks volumes.

Research shows that personal disagreements significantly impair team performance. Task-related disagreements don't. Sometimes they even improve it.

Task-related disagreements usually aren't antagonistic. Everyone's working toward the team goal, but sometimes people disagree about how to get there. A respectful exchange of ideas and perspectives can help us find new ways of thinking. Trouble starts when disrespect and personal judgment enter the chat.

Managing conflict as a leader is hard. People can be fickle, moody, and self-serving. Fundamentally, though, most people want to connect with other people. Leaders who can connect with themselves are more able to connect with others.

Make room in your team structures for members to connect. Don't let disconnection take root. Be there. Listen. Explain and support the mission.

Help your teams foster an environment of respect and appreciation that welcomes differing views. Don't endorse or accept arrogance, superiority, or aggression. Your charge is to create a healthy space for teams to collaborate and thrive as a group and as individuals, with only the occasional task-related conflict.

Team Members

It's not the big conflicts that impede the building of collaborative teams. It's the mistaken idea of what a team really is. It's not just a group of people who work in proximity to one another and have periodic check-ins. That's a work group. Turning groups into teams is a primary mission of the Mindfulness Intelligence corporate training.

The key ingredient for a successful team is a high level of interdependence.

A team that honors interdependence can do innovative and complex things. Teammates rely on each other not just to get their own work done but also to plan, solve problems, and make decisions as a group. A strong team works better at both the group and individual levels when it embraces not just results but personal responsibility, self-awareness, and accountability.

Every team member should:

- Feel safe expressing differing opinions

- Feel safe presenting new options

- Feel that they are good at navigating obstacles

- Have the humility and curiosity to keep learning

- Have a firm conviction that they are a reliable worker

- Care about the well-being of the team and each team member

This is achievable for mentally healthy individuals who are given the opportunity to manage their stress levels and be present in their work and who are not ego-driven drama seekers. That brings us to another big challenge in building healthy teams: High conflict people.

139

High Conflict People

This chapter wouldn't be complete without an examination of one of the biggest and most common challenges to team success: The people who make it nearly impossible to create a collaborative environment. Not just by their own unwillingness or inability to collaborate, but also because they tend to bring out the worst in everyone around them.

We're talking about High Conflict People (HCP). Yes, it's a thing, and it's estimated to be nearly one in every four adults.

"High conflict person" is a personality type, not a psychological diagnosis like narcissistic personality disorder or antisocial disorder. The term was coined by Bill Eddy, who pioneered the High Conflict Personality Theory (HCP) and now runs the High Conflict Institute. If you've ever felt alone in thinking that some people are just impossible to work with, now you know it's such a widespread problem that a whole institute was built around it! If collaboration is the goal, high conflict people must be handled correctly.

Two elements of Eddy's work are particularly helpful: How to identify High Conflict People and how best to deal with them. These tools have helped us recognize people who should be excluded from certain team environments and learn to communicate effectively with HCP without getting sucked into their constant and exhausting drama.

These are the four basic markers of a High Conflict Person:

- They blame others

- They have black-or-white, all-or-nothing thought processes

- They don't manage their emotions well

- They can resort to extreme behavior

It's easy to recognize High Conflict People in business discussions because any problem that's raised has to be someone's fault. HCP jump to negative conclusions based only on their own assumptions. In their black-and-white thinking, there are victims and perpetrators. They want to pin the blame on someone who isn't them.

The odd thing about HCP is that many seem sugar-sweet on the surface. They can appear to be kind and gentle. It draws us in and makes it easy to miss early warning signs. Then they suddenly become emotionally intense, and you recognize the dynamic. HCP are addicted to conflict and emotional upset, so they create it.

High Conflict People will insert distressing things into conversations, sometimes completely out of context because stirring up emotions is part of their playbook. They may do it with a charming demeanor because they need others to emotionally invest in their drama. They want negativity advocates who will condone and amplify their blaming of others. The only time they'll accept blame is if it makes them a martyr. It's tiring for everyone around them.

You'll get a weird gut feeling around a High Conflict Person because you can't really get a bead on them, but you sense that if you don't play their game, they'll find someone else and make you the bad guy. It's easy to feel like an emotional hostage to High Conflict People. You might want to throw some fact-based blame back at them, but that's their end game. Now *you* are the rude one and they will let everybody know it.

High Conflict People have no capacity for self-reflection, so there's little hope they'll change. They will stay in their black-and-white world of blaming others and refuse to look at themselves or take responsibility for their behavior or actions. They sabotage collaboration because they are not interested in finding solutions together. That doesn't fit where they live: The reactive and emotional part of their brain.

As much as our hearts go out to High Conflict People, we can't depend on them to be healthy, long-term members of our business teams. Either they'll have to work alone or everyone around them has to learn how to handle them. Both options limit healthy participation. The only real win you can achieve is by learning to spot High Conflict People before they're hired or managing your communications with those who are thrust upon you.

We're going to tell you about the communication styles to use with High Conflict People, but first, something to keep in mind when you're identifying one. You are not here to judge or condemn. You are not here to establish psychological truths about others. You only want to do a caring assessment of their conflict style so you can learn how best to communicate with them.

Here's a cheat sheet of typical behaviors of High Conflict People:

• Blaming • Black or White reasoning • Unmanaged emotions • Extreme behaviors • Reacts strongly based only on their own assumptions • Recruits negative advocates • Disarming demeanor • No capacity for self-reflection • Makes you feel like an emotional hostage

High Conflict Management

Now that we can identify a High Conflict Person, let's learn how to communicate with them in a business setting. We've put some practices to the test. The two most counterintuitive are:

• Don't apologize.

• Don't give advice.

It's appropriate to apologize to people who are not High Conflict People. It is almost always essential to apologize when we have done or said something hurtful, but High Conflict People are unhealthily focused on naming a villain and an apology will be a basis to blame that person for any or all future events. You can apologize for forgetting to return someone's stapler and the next thing you know you're to blame for the company's reorganization, a drop in sales, and the marketing guy leaving. No, it doesn't make sense, but that's how an overly emotional and reactive HCP operates. You now are to blame for everything, everywhere, all the time.

Giving advice to High Conflict People also tends to backfire. Being in a senior role over a HCP is complicated because any guidance you offer may be perceived as a hostile attack. A High Conflict Person's brain operates from a highly threatened place: The reactive amygdala on the right side (negative emotion) of the limbic system. Your well-meaning advice is not what they hear. Their exaggerated reactions have nothing to do with you. It's how they process and react to information.

Here are some other things that tend to backfire with High Conflict People:

- Don't admonish them

- Don't get into feelings

- Minimize references to the past

No one likes to be reprimanded, but High Conflict People can't bear criticism at any level. Again, this complicates being their boss because when people make mistakes that put other people or the project at risk, they have to be told what didn't work, what they ought to have done instead, and what is expected of them going forward. This very normal business feedback is likely to land with a High Conflict Person like a grenade.

You can't win an emotional argument with a High Conflict Person. If you say something with emotional markers, like *"I'm feeling frustrated that..."* or *"I'm disappointed with..."* or *"It's upsetting to the team when..."* you will receive nonproportional retaliatory fire. After all, no one has it worse than the High Conflict Person! They live in their dark emotions and see the world through a sad, negative lens. You can't win that battle. Don't bring up feelings or emotions.

The best way to sidestep their aversion to criticism and their addiction to stirring up negative emotions is to avoid bringing up the past insofar as you can. HCP hold tightly to their perception of events, and it probably won't even remotely line up with your recollection. Instead, focus on the future.

What Works?

The High Conflict Institute offers a brilliant system for communicating with High Conflict People. It's easy to remember and something we can all do well, especially with some practice. First, let's get our minds and hearts in order for the task.

It's a given that High Conflict People are a drag. They stir up conflict, create drama, *and* have a knack for sabotaging team collaboration. What's not to love, right?

That was just a bit of sarcasm, but it actually brings us to where we were going: The heart. The communication skills we are about to learn have to come from our hearts. This work can't be done from a place of malice. High Conflict People might be high maintenance, but that doesn't mean we shouldn't respect them and even do our best to love them. Assume an attitude of empathy and respect and think "BIFF."

The High Conflict Institute's communication formula is:

- **B**rief

- **I**nformative

- **F**riendly

- **F**irm

Keep your communications with them brief, informative, friendly, and firm to make headway with High Conflict People while protecting your own mental and emotional sphere.

The right kind of brevity is to communicate only what is necessary, in the right means of communication. If you're writing an email, don't be too brief. It will be perceived as terse or hostile. Try to keep digital communications to about five sentences, or a couple of paragraphs at most.

Delivering only information is a good workaround with High Conflict People. It precludes emotional, speculative, defensive language and appeals to their problem-solving capabilities. In brain speak, this approach encourages them to leave their right hindbrain and operate from their left frontal lobe.

Always open and finish close on a friendly note. Don't create opportunities for your intentions to be misinterpreted. Friendly phrases are the bread in a message sandwich: *Thank you for your email.* (Insert meat here). *Have a nice evening.* Be very clear about what you need and when you need it. Don't assume they share your thought processes. If we're not clear about our expectations, we can't be surprised when people don't deliver. It's not about being harsh, it's about being clear. Clarity is kindness! If you need something by a certain date, say so. If you have questions for a High Conflict Person, make them yes or no questions.

Brief. Informative. Friendly. Firm. Used in full this formula can't go wrong. All four elements, no cherry-picking. It even works with people who are not High Conflict People. Stress and pressure assail everyone's nervous systems at some time and can make them temporarily display the traits of High Conflict People. This formula can help you get them through it.

The cardinal rule in dealing with High Conflict People is that you can never, ever, ever tell anyone that you think they are or might be one. Pinky promise? Good.

Back to your own reflections and next steps.

Imagine if everyone at work was trained in how to help a team win. How to trust one another, foster positive relationships, collaborate, resolve conflict, and deal with difficult people. Imagine what future teams could create, innovate, and make happen together. What are your next moves to make your team win?

--

He who experiences the unity of life sees his own Self in all beings, and all beings in his own Self, and looks on everything with an impartial eye.

~ Krishna-Dwaipayana Vyasa, The Bhagavad Gita

--

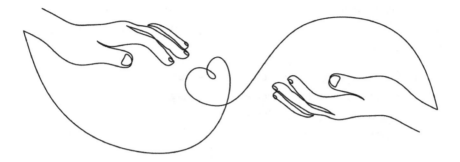

Eleven
Power Sharer

An awareness of power's impact on growth and well-being is key to reaching the big leagues. Power dynamics influence every move in business, but our understanding of them is often limited to our emotional reactions to them.

Most of us can tell when someone is trying to powerplay a room. We can sense it when someone is jealous or suspicious of our power. We can tell when people are sucking up to us to curry favor. It's satisfying to own the power to influence situations, and painful to feel powerless. Many people have big reactions to others' power, especially when that power is abused.

Not many businesspeople think deeply about the meaning of power—what it is, why it's so important, and what their relationship to it is (or should be). That's surprising, considering how central power is to business. Sometimes it feels like it's only about power.

Power tends to be tossed atop a pile of other things like money, titles, and influence. These things are seen as transactional, scored as wins or losses in the struggle to get as many wins as possible.

The instinct to sniff out power, align with it, grab it, and hoard it is an age-old survival mechanism, but one too unrefined to help us in the big leagues. Making a big impact requires sophistication. Just grabbing and hoarding power won't do it.

Both of us have been around corporate power games for decades. It can feel like a constant struggle over who's in charge or who owns the room. Even being caught in the crossfire hurts. As women, we've been targeted by power-tripping men who don't think women belong in the big leagues and by other women who want to protect their own status as a glass-ceiling-breaker. Even if we have ten times their experience and expertise, we have to be prepared to defend our right to exist, because it will be questioned by people who are insecure about their own power piles.

Let's browse through some common misuses of power. We'll examine the nature of power and review some research findings to learn how to navigate a power-hungry business world.

Stephanie: "An eternal power war in the workplace is the practice of policing. Bosses police staff, especially people they don't trust. The rise of remote work has made it both more blatant and more complicated. It's not that I haven't seen healthy decisions made around "return to work" vs. hybrid or remote work, but these decisions often reveal leaders who want to play police. That kind of power play hurts a business more than helps it.

Police officers are among the very few who are authorized to use force against others because sometimes it's needed to maintain public safety. But we're in business, where there is little risk to life, limbs, or property. Do we really trust our employees so little that we feel we have to police them? I've never seen the upside of it. Force creates counterforce. People who feel they're not trusted will rebel against being policed. It's been my experience that if we trust employees to do their jobs and inspire them and give them the resources they need, about 85% will deliver. The ones who abuse the trust will enter a remediation *process or even be fired.*

Policing is an energy killer. It creates resentment and normalizes abuse of trust. Stack that up against managing through a 15% redirection or loss. I'm not saying we should be gullible or wear blinkers. I'm saying we should trust people to do their jobs. A trusting approach is just good business.

A common power play in the big leagues (and beyond) is the use of exclusion tactics that target our primal fear of not belonging. When a targeted person misses important meetings because they were "accidentally" left off the invites or doesn't have answers because neither leaders nor peers are responding to requests for information, assume something's up. This power game is usually meant to make someone give up and leave, or to set them up to be demoted, sent to Siberia, or outright fired. Either way, it becomes impossible for them to perform well. If it's you, keep good documentation so you can't be dismissed for inadequate performance.

There's an unwritten rule in business that bosses are not to be outshined. Why? Aren't we supposed to hire people smarter than we are? Yes, but some bosses are not conscious enough to accept it.

The thing about people in power positions is that they're not always great at their jobs. Some don't have the skills and are threatened by those who do. At the same time, I see many professionals who've attended rah-rah personal empowerment seminars and been told to act like they already have the job they want. I don't think that's great advice. Say a talented professional has a bigger-picture view of a project and sees something the boss hasn't. That advice might lead them to think, "The boss would call this out. I'll bring it up in the next meeting and blow their minds." Workplace power games would likely deliver an immediate smackdown because the boss would have preferred a heads-up rather than to be made to look bad. "Who do you think you are, the CEO?" Acting like you have the job you want can feel threatening to the person who has that job. Show your skills through proactive behaviors that make leadership and the team look good."

Power Flexes

We've seen many professionals shut down and stop contributing when their bright ideas have posed a threat to the power structure. They don't want to be targets themselves or get hit by others' crossfire. We don't condone this approach, but it sometimes happens in the big leagues, so learning about power is essential to becoming powerful.

As big and serious as these power plays are, it usually plays out in the small stuff: Seemingly minor remarks, "innocent" jokes, derogatory comments, "accidental" sabotage, untimely interruptions, or intentional disinterest.

Email is a primary power play tool. Businesspeople use it to posture and try to show others who's boss. The simplest digital communications can send emotions swirling. We've observed some power themes in this area.

<u>Common Email Scenario 1</u>: The big boss sends an email to 20 people on a Saturday afternoon, with questions about a project. Everyone is in the "To" line and no one is directly addressed within the body, so no one knows who should reply. It's the weekend, so people are probably with family or friends when their phones ping. Soccer games, ballet recitals, shopping, dating. The boss is interrupting the personal lives of twenty people. The recipients know they certainly won't be rewarded for ignoring the email until Monday. They might even be admonished or punished. Someone will have to step up. They obsessively refresh their email, further disrupting personal and family time. And because people are out living their lives, chances are the person who replies won't have immediate access to the needed information and will be typing while stressed, distracted, and probably resentful or even angry. In the end, the boss will not only have disturbed everyone's personal time but also set up the responder for failure because that person felt forced to compose their reply from a compromised mental space.

<u>Common Email Scenario 2</u>: The big boss emails a direct report an empty email form with only the subject line "We need to talk." A good outcome rarely follows such a message, so the recipient's brain goes into panic mode. Talk about what? But we have to keep our cool, so we reply, "Sure, what time?" A response doesn't come immediately, and we lose our ability to

concentrate on work or anything else. We wonder if we should call. Anxiety is chewing us up, so we call but it goes to voicemail. Now our minds are spinning with worst-case scenarios. The mental torture ratchets even higher.

A boss on a power trip has no compunction about letting this kind of email hang out there overnight or even through a weekend. Their goal is not to be communicative or fair. It's to brandish their power and show that they're in charge, because if people aren't scared of them, are they even really the boss?

An email that interrupts the weekends of twenty people is a blatant power flex. It would have been easy to indicate who was expected to respond and who wasn't. That's what the "To" and "CC" fields are for. The boss could also have had the courtesy to specify by when they needed a reply, and whether it was an emergency. An empathetic acknowledgement that people's weekends were being interrupted would have been a nice touch too.

But none of that happens in an email that's really just an expression of power.

You may think we're jumping to unfair conclusions about leaders and their intentions. Bosses are busy! People shouldn't be so sensitive! Okay, not everyone has evil intentions, but many just can't control their involuntary power flexes.

Leaders are obligated to consider how their communications will land. If an email isn't meant as a power flex, it takes no extra effort to be clear and compassionate. "We need to talk" is a doom threat in any relationship. If you're writing the email, allude to what it's about and suggest a time and place. Or pick up the phone or jump on a videocall. Better still, just walk over to their office if you can.

Talk to your team about communication styles. An email code of conduct might provide a sense of security. Team members will be more comfortable enjoying life outside work, and the boss can be confident that they'll get the right information from the right person. Best of all, no one will be emotionally exhausted from all the email power-tripping.

Even if you're not the boss, you can demonstrate proper behavior in your own responses. You live on your own timeline and have the right to decide what's important to you. Communicate how and when you'll be able to help.

If you have a boss who will fire you for not answering a non-urgent email on a Saturday, great! It'll be easy to find a better place to work.

Mind Skills

Surprising gifts can come out of an understanding of power in the business world. It becomes easier to handle power dynamics, influence power structures, and recognize how we contribute to the power games ourselves.

Authority

Power and authority are two different things. Your role might carry the authority to make certain decisions or access certain resources. "It's in my power" is a thing we say, but it's really about authority. This contrast isn't splitting hairs. We're steering this mind training into a deeper concept of power that goes beyond titles and authority to the power to influence people and outcomes and make a large, conscious impact on the world.

Caroline Myss, one of the foremost experts on Energy and Archetypes teaches that *every encounter in life is a power negotiation*. We hear this as a call to dig more deeply into our understanding of power.

Force

Leaders who play power games are using force, not power. They choose to "power through" anything regardless of the cost to the project or their team. Being in the realm of physical energy, force often is mistaken as a sign of strength, but its aggressive nature makes it tend to backfire in business.

In David R. Hawkins' brilliant book on consciousness, Power vs. Force, Hawkins concludes that force must always succumb to power because force automatically creates counterforce. He wrote:

"Force always moves against something, whereas power doesn't move against anything at all. Because force has an insatiable appetite, it constantly consumes. Power, in contrast, energizes... and supports. Power gives life and energy—force takes these away. We notice that power is associated with compassion and makes us feel positively about ourselves. Force is associated with judgment and makes us feel poorly about ourselves."

In business, force can present as arrogance and pompousness. Power is characterized by humility and grace. Force polarizes, divides, and repels, while real power attracts and serves others.

Hawkins notes: *"Force needs to control others because it lacks power, just as vanity stems from a lack of self-esteem."*

Energy

The best way to understand power is to separate it from authority and force and instead perceive it as a dynamic energy. Power and energy can't be fully equated, because while power can be infinite, energy is always finite in that it can't be created or destroyed. It can only transform.

Clara Moscowitz at Scientific American writes: *"We now know that the universe is expanding at a faster and faster rate—propelled by something scientists call dark energy. This is thought to be the intrinsic energy per cubic centimeter of empty space. But if the universe is a closed system with a finite amount of energy, how can it spawn more empty space, which must contain more intrinsic energy, without creating additional energy? It turns out that in Einstein's theory of general relativity, regions of space with positive energy actually push space outward. As space expands, it releases stored-up gravitational potential energy, which converts into the intrinsic energy that fills the newly created volume. So even the expansion of the universe is controlled by the law of energy conservation."*

That paragraph covers dark energy, positive energy, intrinsic energy, and stored-up potential energy. Your biggest energy emitters are your emotions. Calm emits more powerful energy than aggression. Joy carries more energy than boredom. Satisfaction measures stronger than envy.

Energy moves everything in business and leadership. We may encounter flowy, easy, uplifting energy or creepy, bullying, scary energy. Understanding energy's various guises will help us in power negotiations.

Transaction

Power in business is seen as transactional. If I get some, you lose some. If I give it to you, I have none left. If I have power and you get more than I have, I have lost. It's a finite game. We see this dynamic in play when businesspeople hoard their power and jockey for more. It's hard to watch, mainly because it's so ineffective.

We sometimes see businesspeople hoarding information because they think, consciously or unconsciously, that being the only one "in the know" will bring them power. This thinking is backward. Sharing information expands power.

Some people base every move on the pursuit of power because they think it will help them advance their careers. Again, this is backward. It will lead to a cycle of ego rising to meet other people's ego moves. A push for power is a use of force, and force always leads to counterforce.

Power Expansion

Think of power as a lit torch. Protect your own flame and use it to kindle another's torch. Sharing is caring. Teams who feel cared for will support their leader more fully and produce better results.

The notion of empowering others is not new in the leadership world. What is new is how critical it has become to success.

You can't make great things happen without supportive teams, and you can't afford to be slowed down by the counterforces that self-serving leadership elicits. Share your power and watch it expand.

Power Over vs. Power With

Global research leader Just Associates conducted an in-depth study of power in the workplace, analyzing 60,000 data points over twenty years. Its conclusions resonate deeply with our own experience.

Typical workplace power games fall into one of two categories: A control factor for gain, or a change agent for good. The former relies on "power over," while the latter is based on "power with/within."

Power games—at work, at home, anywhere—suck us into a destructive system. If we can identify the type of power play that's at hand, we can take steps to address it within ourselves and in our teams.

Power Over

The old business paradigm is based on bosses having "power over" people. How else to get people to do what we tell them? This approach treats power as a zero-sum game. If someone doesn't acquire and hang onto power, then someone else will have power over them. People stuck in "power over" mode view every move and encounter through this lens.

1. If you show weakness, others will use it against you.

2. If you show strength, others will try to override you, outdo you, or enlist you so they can then turn the tables and beat you.

Those are the only two choices in the "power over" world. The Just Associates research found that "power over" types construed things like kindness, compassion, humility, and service as signs of weakness, of a "loser." "Power over" types use dehumanizing strategies and language, which means they're aware at some level of the inherent power in those human qualities. Devaluing decency is the most efficient and effective way to destabilize people and societies to maintain a "power over" position.

Victimhood is a more subtle way of acquiring "power over." Victims tend to be seen as not accountable and maybe even weak, but victimhood can be used to leverage people's fear. A victim offloads responsibility by pointing a finger while appealing to people's natural impulse to rescue others. That's how victims get their way.

People who want to have power over others will leverage fear to get and keep it.

Shame, blame, and bullying are the underlying themes of the "power over" leadership style, whether it comes as a public reaming or just a nasty email. Sowing division and insecurity are how these types show people who's boss. Why? Because it's much easier to hold power over people who are divided and insecure.

But establishing a culture of fear is the opposite of good leadership.

If you have ever wondered how a leader can be so cruel and inhumane, know that when someone is trying to maintain "power over," the cruelty is the point. It's the most effective way to stimulate our old fears of humiliation and exclusion and make us fold.

Some leaders can't bear to be criticized or questioned themselves, so they arrange to have only yes-people around them. They get away with it because many organizations themselves rely on a "power over" structure and have built large systems to protect it.

We're seeing encouraging signs of change, though. Organizations with healthier power structures and empathy-driven values are outperforming companies that still operate in the old paradigm. Large companies whose success is based on their industry footprint are realizing that they'll have to become more innovative and responsive.

The leaders who will shape the future are those who seek "power with."

Power With

The best kind of power is "power with." This school of thought posits that power is infinite, that rather than needing to be hoarded, it grows when shared.

When we see the good in people, choose to trust them, and agree to

collaborate, it brings more power to our projects.

Leading from a position of "power with" creates the emotional stability people need to function as brilliant geniuses or great team members. That stability is strengthened when people feel valued individually and unified as a team. It elevates everyone's performance and contribution. In this power paradigm, decency is foundational for decision-making. "Power with" is a change agent for good.

The leadership style of "power with" is one that embraces belonging, goodness, and diverse viewpoints, even criticism. We're not saying business is a fantasy world of cupcakes and rainbows. "Power with" works because it also requires accountability and an openness to discomfort.

When people are allowed to criticize and disagree, things will sometimes turn uncomfortable. When we commit to accountability, we're sure to learn hard truths about ourselves. There is no way around the discomfort if we want to experience the connection and belonging that form empathy-driven values and agendas. That's where great work will come from.

"Power with" goes hand in hand with "power within." Leaders have an obligation to give people the room and resources for a constructive personal growth path that leads to the emotional maturity they'll need to succeed and become empowered leaders themselves.

Sharing power honors the third branch on the "power with" tree, which is "power to." When we give power to our teams to do their jobs well and stay connected to their own power, we are sharing our power.

Leadership that's based on "power with," "power to," and "power within" is the most effective way to build a culture of learning that leads to successful teamwork.

Most people will agree that these are the more appealing styles of power. "Power with" is influential rather than forceful. It helps us live with meaningful purpose instead of being a self-serving jerk. Who would prefer the awful behaviors and ultimate futility of the "power over" approach?

Why, the ego, of course.

Our ego inclines us to choose "power over." After all, power is the ego's favorite game. Ego-driven behavior provokes other egos to respond with either retaliation or surrender. Don't give in to it.

Navigating

Insight into these diametrically opposed approaches will help you make healthier choices around power. That includes deciding whom you want to work for and what kind of culture will best support your mission.

It's hard to navigate a culture of "power over" with serenity and grace. It feels impossible to counter bullies with acts of kindness and generosity. Perhaps it's time to choose a different environment. First, let's make sure we're not taking any toxic behaviors with us. Yes, it's possible that we've picked up (or fallen back into) bad habits without even noticing. It's deeply disappointing to discover that we ourselves might be the controlling bulldozer or victimhood manipulator who abuses a position of power. It's disturbing to recognize our own undermining behaviors being mirrored by others.

Let's unpack that in the only place we have control of our power: Within.

Power Within

Your "power within" is a reflective space where you can question yourself, feel into your own truth and alignment, and find your own empowerment. That may seem like a lot of "you" and "your," but it's not selfish to start from within. You can't empower others until your own stuff is in order.

This book is about how to connect with the authentic power within you so you can truly connect with people and opportunities. Let's reflect on our own relationship to power.

- What drives me to lead teams and projects the way I do?

    o Do I lead on autopilot, or am I intentional in my leadership? How do I know the difference?

    o Do I react with "power over" behavior when confronted by

"power over" people? These behaviors might be arrogance, vengeance, blame, belittling, gossiping, or any form of dehumanization. What is my go-to response in these situations?

- o Am I stuck on a certain track or timeline because I'm convinced that it will make me look good, smart, promotable?

- How do I hold myself accountable?

- o Have I made it clear to my closest confidants that they should call me on my bullshit?

- o Have I really listened to the people around me? Have I paid attention to experts? Have I heard the team's grumblings?

- o Am I clear on my values (my *Who*) and my mission (my *Why*), and do I live in integrity with both?

- How does stress, pressure, or overwhelm change me?

- o Do I become single-minded? (Rigid, not open, not listening)

- o Do behaviors like overconfidence and self-importance emerge?

- o Do I operate from fear and desperation? (Moody, angry, rash, indifferent)

So many things can drain our energy and make us feel like we're losing our power. Trying to disguise our own flaws is one of them.

Now is the time to be big enough to deal with the dark stuff: Negative emotions, shadows, shame. Finding things that we're not proud of in ourselves shouldn't make us feel bad. Every human has light and shadows within them. As adults who want to be powerful and empowering changemakers, we have to be brave and look at the dark stuff too. Remember, repressed or suppressed negative emotions will always be transferred or projected elsewhere. *I can't stand these painful emotions so here, you take them.* Instead of spreading light, we spread pain. Until we stop shying away from the hard stuff.

It's time to take responsibility and acknowledge things we'd rather not. In being lovingly present with our dark spots, we heal them and transcend them. When we work on our wholeness, we meet the authentic and powerful leader we've always wanted to be.

These are big life concepts with significant implications, but as with many big things, it starts with the small:

- Connecting with your stillness and truth on a daily basis

- Practicing not taking things personally

- Being connected to the bigger picture

- Choosing thoughts and feelings that serve your mission

- Remembering that how you show up inspires people to match your level

- Encouraging your teams to work on their personal growth as well

As we examine what strengthens and diminishes our own power, we can assess the degree to which our minds are cleaned and healed. Refer back to the *Be the Cleaner* chapter for more ways to become empowered.

One more thing: Power within doesn't come just from taking care of your mind. Take care of your body as well. It's easy to say that we need to eat well and get plenty of sleep and exercise, but harder to do, especially when we have lost our connection with our physical selves. Two of our favorite ways to reconnect are mindfulness walking meditation and tai chi.

Attending to your physical needs is a beautiful act of self-care and empowerment. Physical fitness will improve your stamina and generate positive power in your personal and career endeavors.

Sharing Power

As we understand more about power—authority, force, energy; power over, with, to, and within—we grow our skill at navigating its perils and begin enjoying the expansive experience of sharing power.

In the workplace, one of the greatest benefits of power sharing is the learning culture it creates. A culture of eager learners is absolutely vital for success.

Many business projects are kicked off without every conceivable detail having been forecast. Things move so fast that information or innovations might not yet be known or available. You need your teams to be capable of learning—and of learning fast so they can turn on a dime to support needs.

Sharing your power will help your teams become great learners.

A platform for shared power will come with ups and downs and victories and defeats. There will be joyous moments and hard ones too. But you'll have the shared excitement of making the world a better place together. What a spectacular reason to be a power-sharing leader in business.

--

In the universe, there are things that are known, and things that are unknown, and in between, there are doors.

~ William Blake

--

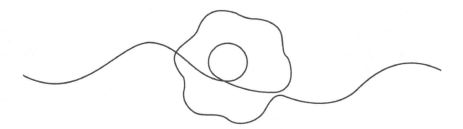

Twelve
Unscrambled Eggs

Leadership demands constant transformation in people and processes. Maybe "business" should be spelled C-H-A-N-G-E. There's always a need to update, alter, modify, improve, and make better, to think beyond what has been thought before and find solutions. As exhausting as it can be for everyone, it's how leaders stay ahead.

Sometimes a thing will happen that's of an even higher amplitude than our already transformation-oriented leadership lives. Something unexpected, possibly beyond our capabilities, becomes an irreversible reality. This kind of change can be described as *transmutation*. Just as it's impossible to unscramble an egg or put a butterfly back in its cocoon, transmutation creates irrevocable change.

Leaders stay relevant by upskilling to meet our transmutational times.

If you think technological advances like artificial intelligence don't affect you then you're not paying attention. If you don't think we all need to plan today for the best use of technology tomorrow, you underestimate your part in the evolutionary process.

Technology is yet again asking leaders to assume new shapes, level up, and be ready for the next level of human evolution.

Stephanie: *"A while back my husband and I decided to take up Tai Chi. He had previously attended classes under Grand Master Willie Lim, but I was a rookie. We found an authentic teacher near our home and jumped right in.*

I was pleasantly surprised to discover that Tai Chi aligned very well with my daily meditation practice. Tai Chi and Qigong are moving meditations that cultivate your life force, your Chi. Classes are designed to connect your own essence with the group's energy, and ultimately the universe's energetic essence. Imagine a group of adults wearing bright-yellow t-shirts and baggy gold pants, all lined up on gym mats and moving in unison. I loved it immediately (loud, baggy attire notwithstanding).

One recent weekday I had spent most of my day on calls. One with executives at a company I advise, another with the CEO of a startup I'm involved in, and a group call for women executives that Linda hosts each week. Every call eventually turned to the hot topic of artificial intelligence and its business possibilities and potential.

That same day, I watched an interview with "grandfather of AI" Geoffrey Hinton. Hinton left an executive position at Google to be free to air his views and concerns about AI. I also caught a YouTube clip of MIT scientist and researcher Lex Fridman interviewing OpenAI founder Sam Altman about the technological aspects of generative AI. Both conversations addressed the social and human impacts of AI as well as the business ramifications.

My business day closed with a catch-up call with a former Charter colleague. We had a great conversation about... you guessed it! AI.

After AI had eaten my day, I left early for a Tai Chi class, stopping first to visit my parents. They were the first people I'd spoken to all day who didn't bring up AI.

That night our teacher, Shi Fu Gregg, held class outdoors...in the parking lot. Not terribly glamorous, but the fresh air was nice. We must have been a sight in our puffy yellow clothing.

During the class's meditation segments, the teacher gives verbal prompts to help us sync our movements and breathing. Inhale on the upward movements; exhale as we slowly sink down. He also assists visualization by instructing us to feel the energy in and around us and connect to universal energy. It's incredibly soothing and makes me feel very connected to myself and all things.

Everyone in the class seemed to be having their own unique experience of the energy field. I let my lingering thoughts about AI flow through my movements. Separate machines sharing intelligence through a network of data and prompts. As I compared my understanding of AI, networks, and connected machines to the reality of being connected to the group in my Tai Chi class, I felt the similarities—but even more strongly, the stark differences. Machines that use AI don't have a nervous system. They can't love or feel joy. No matter how well AI learns to simulate human behavior, machines don't have empathy. They can only appear to have empathy. They can display kindness, but they are not kind. They can outperform us at a multitude of tasks, including complex thinking, but that has nothing on the sweet complexity of being human and feeling that life is rich and full of love. They can't even be scared or pissed off.

When I got home that night, I did what any normal person would have done. I asked ChatGPT: How are you doing today?

ChatGPT: *As an AI, I don't have emotions or physical sensations, so I don't experience "good" or "bad" days. However, I'm here and ready to assist you with any questions or tasks you have. How can I help you today?*

Me: *Do you think you are conscious?*

ChatGPT: *As an AI language model, I do not possess consciousness or self-awareness. While I can generate responses and interact with users,*

I lack subjective experiences, emotions, and consciousness. I operate based on patterns and algorithms designed to process and generate human-like text based on the input I receive.

I thought to myself, now we know! It can't even choose to put on a loud baggy outfit and go do Tai Chi.

I am in no way making light of the fact that AI will require us to be accountable for its use. Many experts believe we are at a watershed moment in technological history. Humans will be tested once again."

Mind Skills

Technological advances are coming along at breakneck speed, and it's important to be prepared for an accompanying shift in human consciousness. If technology becomes an arms race among companies that don't have solid principles and good foresight, the consequences could be dire.

It's time for the business world to recognize the impact of our actions on the planet—and beyond—and move from a mindset of exploitation and overconsumption toward one of stewardship and regeneration. It's time to rethink our economic systems, our modes of production and consumption, and our relationship with the natural world. It's time to acknowledge the interconnectedness of all living things. Leaders need a holistic understanding of well-being that's based on social connections, community, and a sense of purpose, with space for an abundance of achievement and progress—and, yes, wealth.

This consciousness shift will require a deep commitment to personal growth and self-reflection and a willingness to engage in dialogue and collaboration. It won't happen overnight. Ensuring an abundant future will take constant effort and willingness to challenge our assumptions, beliefs, and systems.

What's in it for you? You'll be a conscious, impactful leader who helps shape the world to be more inclusive, abundant, and sustainable.

Let's examine the complex coalescence of technological advancement, what it means to be human, and the fate of evolution by looking at the top three areas that can help you bring positive change to the universe: Self-Awareness, When Reality Shifts, and Your Decisions Matter.

Self-Awareness

Self-awareness is the golden portal to successful leadership in transmutational times. It frees leaders from the burden of past worries and future anxieties and helps them maintain a strong connection to a co-creative vision of the future. Ironically, this can only happen within the present moment. We call this the Past-Future paradox.

The Past–Future Paradox

Advice like "Don't live in the past BUT acknowledge and honor it to heal" sounds like a paradox itself. So does "Don't leap into the future BUT stay connected to your vision of it." Both are true, but we can experience and process only the present moment.

As discussed earlier in this book, the nervous system works like a time machine. Old subconscious programming triggers outsized reactions to small situations. Without the right mind skills, our early programming will dictate our future. We offer these insights and tools to help you find your healed, present-moment power and keep an intentional gaze on the future. Connecting, noticing, healing, and adjusting are the heart of self-awareness.

Let's go where it may sting: Managers and leaders tend to lean too heavily on past achievements to support their value. Business and leadership training has taught us that we should brandish our achievements so people will be impressed and respect us. The challenge now is that in this sped-up world, our previous accomplishments seem farther behind us.

*Be proud of your achievements and honor yourself for having met **those** moments. Now it's time to meet the current moment and evolved leaders won't be asking about what you've done in the past. They'll ask how it's prepared you for a new role, project, or task.*

Businesses rely on performance metrics, but even when done in service of predicting future patterns and flows it's still old news, old data, old manifestations. There's also such a thing as too much data. A leader can't rely on old information to make quick, complex, and correct decisions for the future. You have to be the visionary who sees what's ahead.

Good information supports better decision-making. Connecting to evolutionary intelligence goes beyond metrics or measurement, and it happens through self-awareness.

Self-awareness means being connected to your consciousness. The portal is within you but what you experience goes far beyond that. When you experience awareness through yourself you become aware of the energy field that creates everything and connects everyone.

Two categories of leaders have the most difficulty finding their connection with the future.

1. Those who think everything is moving too fast, who keep looking back and allowing the past to dictate the future. All they want is to feel safe and get it right, but they exude a fearful, insecure kind of energy. They tend to carry a lot of stress but will often pretend nothing's wrong.

2. Those who thrive on the exhilaration of change but are not fully present in key moments of decision-making. They may see themselves as bold and assertive but their energy feels like they're trying to outrun uncomfortable feelings—often straight off a cliff. They recover fast, but you can only do that so many times.

When you slip away from the present moment you limit your power. A presence practice like meditation will calm your nervous system and allow you to operate from a deep state of awareness, connecting to wisdom beyond yourself.

Self-awareness is rooted in the ability to be present. In presence, you can suspend your ego, sense how you impact a room, and be awake and alert to connect to possibilities—both present and future.

Becoming Obsolete

In the big leagues, your self-awareness will allow you to advance farther and faster.

In the film Gladiator, Emperor Marcus Aurelius tells General Maximus that he wants Maximus to succeed him when he dies rather than let primogeniture assign the crown to his evil son Commodus. Maximus is honored but respectfully declines, saying he doesn't want to become Emperor. "That's why it has to be you," Marcus Aurelius replies.

Your life may not feel like a Hollywood movie but a Hero's Journey is a Hero's Journey. You are called to cross over a threshold into another world where you meet new friends and new foes, fight dragons in the abyss, learn lessons, and return home with new gifts.

In the business world, the "abyss" is to become obsolete. Irrelevant. Unwanted. These words hurt! Now imagine yourself as the hero in Gladiator. "*I don't want to become obsolete,*" you say. "*That's why you have to become obsolete,*" comes the reply.

That's the paradox. As much as you fight the idea of being replaced, people will find you more appealing than ever when you've accepted the possibility of obsolescence. Throw off the fear and you can dictate your own choices and leave situations that don't serve you. Bonus: Other people won't be able to manipulate you, so you can do the bigger things you are meant to do while team members also have opportunities to step up and perform at their highest levels. That is self-awareness in its best form.

When Reality Shifts

Most transmutational events in the modern day are set off by technological advances. Telephones and television changed everything. Now we have smartphones and virtual-reality headsets and, of course, artificial intelligence. It's changed our perception of what's true or even real. We can't tell anymore whether a video is genuine, or if reporting is reliable, or that a piece of art was made by a human hand.

When we can't believe our own eyes and ears, it's hard to know what is true. That kind of confusion can lead to conflict, infighting, and division. Clarity and communication, especially from leaders, are paramount. No AI can replace a leader who can shepherd teams through times of difficulty, fear, and uncertainty and take strategic actions based on their own experience and expertise.

The COVID-19 pandemic is another example of a transmutational event. It was the perfect storm for a reality shift. It impacted virtually everyone on Earth and created such immense change that the separation will always be there: Before COVID, since COVID.

When the world went home in early 2020, companies had to focus on their technology roadmaps and figure out how to deliver, both literally and figuratively. Employees had to have the equipment to work remotely. Product still had to be shipped out. Logistics vulnerabilities and supply chain challenges threw many operations into a panic.

Managing or working on teams took on a more human element. Meetings—conducted via videocall—didn't dive right into agendas. Rather, people checked in with one another, asking caring questions like *How are you doing? Are your mom and dad okay? Kids home? Do you need anything?* Fear and anxiety were out in the open in the workplace and for once that was okay.

At the same time, businesses had to develop policies and processes to support huge and disparate workforces.

Managers had to learn how to lead remote employees in ways that respect their personhood.

Some companies now are mandating a return to the office. It's not going terribly well. People's priorities have shifted, especially those of younger employees and parents of young children. They've now had several years to notice that replacing commuting time with family or personal time contributes to their wellness, happiness, and success. Leaders will have to figure out how to go forward in this new reality in a way that doesn't lead to talent exits.

What Is Real?

Keanu Reeves recounted a recent conversation with a teenager who asked him about his 1999 film The Matrix. "There's this guy who's in a kind of virtual world," Reeves told her. "And he finds out that there's a real world, and he's really questioning what's real and what's not real. And he really wants to know what's real." The teen's response surprised him. "Why? Who cares if it's real?"

Younger minds may have a different view of reality and truth. As we've mentioned, the human nervous system just isn't great at distinguishing real from fake. We're very easy to manipulate. Now that technological advancements continue to make "truth" ever more fungible, leaders can't afford to be easily manipulated. Conscious leaders in transmutational times need clear, calm, highly discerning minds.

Just a couple of years ago, most of us thought that unskilled, repetitive, low-paying jobs would be the first to be lost to robots and AI. But instead, AI is jockeying for sophisticated and creative jobs, even ones that historically have required higher education.

Until recently, juries for the most prestigious photography and art awards insisted they could spot AI-generated art a mile away. Then in 2023 German photographer Boris Eldagsen declined a Sony World Photography award and announced that his prizewinning entry had been generated through artificial intelligence prompts. In a statement, he described himself as a "cheeky monkey" and said he'd meant the submission as a stunt to bring attention to the downside of using AI in photography.

We'll see more disputes around this. Comedian Sarah Silverman already has sued OpenAI for using her copyrighted intellectual property to train AI. At the time of this writing, both the actors' union SAG-AFTRA and the Writers Guild of America are on strike, partly to protest the use of their likenesses and work in AI-generated content.

Beyond art and entertainment, some AI programs have been able to pass the U.S. Medical Licensing Examination. Dr. Roboto will see you now!

Your Decisions Matter

The world and humanity will face numerous challenges in the upcoming decades as new, as-yet unimaginable technologies enter our lives. Even if you don't work in the tech industry, technological solutions are likely to play an increasing part in your core business. You need a skilled mind to make sound decisions.

Just as the flutter of a butterfly's wing can initiate a hurricane, you live at the inflection point of your decisions. You already know that what you do matters. Take the next step and embrace the power of your thoughts and feelings. Your energy and intention will have implications on the future for you, for us, and for the world.

Rearview Mirror

When we drive forward as leaders, it's smart to glance at the rearview mirrors. It helps us recall what we've passed and understand how we got here.

Innovation plays a pivotal role in shaping our paths whether the intentions and outcomes are positive or negative. It's on leaders to evaluate any innovative endeavor's potential impact on humanity and anticipate and mitigate potential harm. Conscious decisions will need to be made about timing, safety, and even futility.

The invention of the atomic bomb ushered in the Nuclear Age and had an immediate and significant impact on global politics and world events. For the first time, our ability to destroy had surpassed our power to create. This pivotal development fundamentally altered the human psyche by instilling in us a new level of existential fear. This in turn prompted new coping mechanisms against the profound implications of this new reality.

The advent of the internet brought about a sweeping evolutionary transformation. Global information accessibility altered the way we communicate, learn, and work. It has reshaped our social interactions and allowed us to form relationships, build communities, and connect with like-minded individuals we'd never otherwise have met. But the internet has also introduced new types of crimes and provided a global stage for bullying, intimidation, and hate. Additionally, isolation and loneliness have contributed to mental health issues at a level we haven't seen before.

Adding wireless technology to internet capability was like throwing gasoline on a fire. Social media and virtual reality can bring wonderful opportunities, but they also contribute to increased levels of anxiety, depression, and fear. Our sense of reality becomes warped. Smartphones with their fun games and apps have proven addictive, especially for kids and young adults. Our new tech habits interrupt family time, diminish our attention spans, and disrupt our sleep. Unintended or overlooked consequences are everywhere. The fact that a large segment of the workforce prefers to work remotely speaks volumes about the change in the value of social interaction.

Leaders face more challenges around mind skills and well-being than they did a decade ago.

We're certainly not saying technological developments are bad. We're saying people change in response to them, which necessitates greater awareness and new types of training.

People are remarkably adaptable to new realities. Healthy minds find ways to balance the benefits of technology with physical, mental, emotional, and spiritual needs. We hope you've developed habits and routines to manage your digital life—including occasionally unplugging—and that you encourage your teams to do the same.

Decisions made today in the normal course of business can impact the future in ways we can't yet imagine. We've still got to do our best, because as technology and automation continue to integrate into our everyday lives, we will have to live with our past decisions.

The development and deployment of innovations is akin to building a house: It relies on a strong foundation. Answering some deep questions will help that foundation last longer than any digital fad or technical trend. Examine your intentions, values, and ethics. Ask your teams to do the same. Make sure everyone is aligned and grounded, their minds freed of old junk. Give yourself and others room to recalibrate to stay on course toward the future vision.

Leadership Upgrade

Leadership has been understood to be the process of guiding and directing others toward the company's goal or vision. Effective leaders are often defined as people with strong decision-making and strategic thinking skills and an ability to motivate others.

These traits and qualities no longer are sufficient on their own.

The business world is beginning to realize it needs people who excel at the human side of leadership. This is apparent from the way the adoption of digital technology has been accompanied by an intensified focus on ESG (Environmental, Social, and Governance) and DEI (Diversity, Equity, and Inclusion). This new outlook significantly changes the nature of leadership.

Leaders must understand the potential human impact of the technology they unleash on humanity.

As your self-awareness grows and you adapt to the rapid shifts in perceived reality, you want to avoid a future of trying to unscramble eggs or teaching others how to do it. Here are some leadership upgrades to consider in these transmutational times:

1. **Industry Know-How -- > Digital Literacy**
    Industry knowledge no longer is your most valuable asset. Embracing, understanding, and being able to navigate complex digital ecosystems including data analytics, social media, and AI-powered tools now are just table stakes. Great leaders must be able to harness the power of relevant technologies to drive innovation and create value for their organizations.

2. **Strategic Thinking -- > Strategic Connection**
    Complex digital ecosystems and vast datasets require leaders to step up their creative and strategic thinking. It's no longer enough to crank out short-term fixes. The most effective leaders

will harness their own self-awareness to connect the dots between vision, people, consciousness, possibilities, and learning.

3. **Collaborative Silos -- > Inclusive Co-creation**
   Collaboration is key in an interconnected world. Leaders now have to take it a step further. If we are to create smart solutions for the world, the world must be part of the conversation. Invite members of different cultures, ethnicities, orientations, and circumstances, including the neurodiverse. Inclusivity and openness to different perspectives lead to better, more impactful outcomes.

4. **Change Management -- > Agile Identity**
   Change management teaches that leaders need to adapt quickly to new technologies, market conditions, and other factors, but things now move too fast to do it in a controlled, linear way. It's no longer about *handling* change, it's about *being* the change. Leaders have to maintain agility to operate freely in the present moment while keeping a curious eye on the future.

5. **Emotional Intelligence -- > Mindfulness Intelligence**
   The ability to be conscious and mindful is what sets humans apart from even the most sophisticated AI. As leaders, we value emotional intelligence (EQ) and promote those who are emotionally mature. Managing psychology and emotions is no longer enough. Leaders need mindfulness intelligence (MQ) in order to succeed.

The digital transmutation of leadership as we've known it will continue as technology advances in tandem with human evolution. Leaders must be willing to adapt and learn as the needed skills and competencies for effective leadership continue to shift. One thing is clear: The human element of leadership will always be key no matter how advanced our technologies become.

The most successful leaders will be those who can balance their technological skills with their understanding of self and their ability to connect

with others.

Ethical and responsible use of technology should be a top priority for leaders. Every new piece of tech requires mindful assessments of its potential impacts on people and society. Policies and guidelines must be developed to address and mitigate negative consequences.

We know it can be exhausting to keep up with technology. But when you're a leader who is aligned and present, sure of your values, and connected to the pulse of evolutionary intelligence, you are prepared to make the best possible decisions.

--

"If you want to find the secrets of the universe, think in terms of energy, frequency and vibration."

~ Nikola Tesla

--

Thirteen
Notes for The Road

You're in the home stretch of your mind skills journey. Let a visionary technologist and a consciousness expert give you some bonus insights about being an effective, conscious leader who understands technology's pitfalls and potential.

Let's explore the intersection of transmutational technology and human consciousness as it relates to leadership in the big leagues.

Mitchko: Technology Notes for The Road

Leaders make an enormous mistake to think they're not affected by technological advancements. Tech influences every aspect of how we live our personal lives and conduct our business, and ignoring that stubborn fact leads only to faulty decisions and lost opportunities. I've spent more than 25 years in tech, including in C-suites, observing the ever-changing landscape of tech. Here are my best pro tips for growing into a more discerning executive, one who knows the right questions to ask in navigating the tech world.

First of all: Practice and use the mind skills you've learned from this book. Tech evolves and deploys at a frenetic pace. A calm and ordered mind will help you operate at your peak.

Secondly, do everything you can to make useful technologies widely accessible. A top goal would be in helping to bring broadband service to underserved communities so everyone can access the resources and tools to succeed in a rapidly changing world.

Here are some key technologies to learn about and monitor:

1. **Artificial Intelligence (AI) advancements:** AI had been a part of our lives on some level for a while before its sudden exponential growth made it explode into our culture. Natural language processing, computer vision, and machine learning are used in applications ranging from virtual assistants and autonomous vehicles to personalized marketing communications and healthcare diagnostics. The technology is not without controversy: As of this writing, more than 30,000 executives and leaders in the AI space have united to recommend pausing AI commercialization until the tech is better understood. It's imperative to learn and understand the role AI plays in your company and industry, and in the life and work of you and your teams.

2. **5G Technology:** The rollout of 5G (fifth generation) wireless technology is cranking along in many parts of the world. Promising faster download and upload speeds, lower latency, and increased connectivity, 5G has the potential to revolutionize industries like telecommunications, transportation, and the Internet of Things (IoT). Look into how deploying 5G tech can help the communities you serve or want to serve.

3. **Internet of Things (IoT) Growth:** IoT represents the interconnectivity of devices and objects via the internet, from smart homes

and wearable devices to industrial automation and smart cities. The IoT continues to expand and is transforming various industries by improving efficiency, convenience, and sustainability. Stay aware of IoT's progress so you can improve your products and business.

4. **Blockchain and Cryptocurrencies:** Blockchain technology enables decentralized and secure financial transactions. It forms the basis for cryptocurrencies like Bitcoin and Ethereum that have gained significant traction as digital assets and investment opportunities. Before you jump onto that bandwagon, though, think about how blockchain would support your goal, consider the potential environmental ramifications, and consider the feasibility of integrating the tech into your business model.

5. **Biotechnology and Genetic Editing:** New gene editing technologies like CRISPR-Cas9 have opened up new vistas for genetic modification and manipulation. This tech has potential in areas including healthcare, agriculture, and environmental conservation. It might cure diseases and eradicate illness, but it might also be used for purposes that are detrimental to society and to evolution. Scientific and ethical considerations are still being discussed nearly two decades after the technology was introduced.

If you think artificial intelligence is way out there, just wait until it's successfully paired with quantum computing and CRISPR. We haven't seen anything yet.

I'm a big fan of AI, machine learning, and automation. I've long relied on these tools to eliminate tedious functions, automate systems management, and forecast and execute preventative maintenance. I'm not here to get you stressed or stir up your Fear of Missing Out. You don't have to put every new tech at the top of your priority list. Just know that leaders can no longer look at a list like this and think *So what's that got to do with me?*

We are all technologists now whether we like it or not.

Technology is everywhere, no matter who you are or where you work. All industries are pairing up with technology partners to innovate, improve and expand the way they do business.

I recently attended one of the healthcare industry's largest trade shows. Prestigious industry leaders gave speeches about technology being the solution to many healthcare challenges. One panel featured the World Economic Forum's head of AI/Machine Learning, a vice president of research from Microsoft, and the Mayo Clinic's Chief Information Officer. The topic they explored was—you see this coming now, right?—how artificial intelligence fits into the world of healthcare delivery.

Ask yourself the same question about your own industry. Get ahead of potential downsides and unintended consequences. What do you need to know about it? How can you harness its power without doing harm? What are people afraid of? Is there merit to feelings of unease? What other conversations must be had to diminish potential risks? What ethical and legal implications should be discussed? What does it mean to be human when you are living and working beside this technology?

The topic of AI and its capabilities and potential are everywhere, as usually happens with great advancements in tech, but this time is different. AI technology is too sophisticated to be tested and monitored with traditional tools. New industry-specific metrics and procedures will have to be developed. Every industry will encounter its own unique opportunities and challenges around these tools. Only by being informed, engaged, and proactive can we ensure that technology is a force for positive change, not a destroyer. We can't rely solely on policymaking, either. We have to shift our collective consciousness to prioritizing sustainability, equity, and long-term thinking.

To lead in a world that already has AI embedded in daily life, you need to ask a lot of questions. Tech moves fast, but some questions still will have to be asked, answered, and understood as technology evolves:

- *Is the platform I am using secure?*
  Cybersecurity likely is already part of the way you keep your data and systems safe. Keep doing what you can to keep your systems safe as AI evolves. Keep in mind that most models will require live data, so make sure that's in the discussions and processes regarding breaches.

Become good friends with your CISO or IT leads. They'll have to develop clear security guidelines and ensure everyone using your systems knows about risks.

- **What datasets was the model trained on?**
  Most open-source models have been trained on publicly available datasets like Wikipedia entries, news articles, books, and magazines. When you use a model, or have a vendor integrate AI capabilities in your application, you may be using another company's proprietary data. Know what data is being used and how.

- **Are there intrinsic biases in the data?**
  A thousand times YES! Accuracy, transparency, and user rights are key issues that should be discussed by cross-departmental teams, and not just the group that's responsible for privacy. AI knows only what we tell it, so monitor for intrinsic biases that perpetuate inaccuracies and injustices toward minority, or marginalized, individuals and groups.

- **Is the data meeting your privacy regulations?**
  Depending on where you do business, topics, and legislation like GDPR, LGPD PIPEDA, and the NIST Privacy Framework must be taken into consideration. Make sure that you or your organization develop and maintain a comprehensive list of relevant items so your organization can adhere to mandated privacy laws and standards.

- **What are the consequences if the model makes a bad decision?**
  Outcomes could range from inconvenient to catastrophic, so this is a very important question. An algorithm-created marketing list built around the wrong demographic target might cost your company some money or negatively impact your brand, but an automated medical assistant giving flawed medication information could be devastating. Perform an intensive risk analysis before implementing a system. Use your imagination and your industry knowledge to identify and assess potentially problematic situations. Put the right controls in place early on.

- **In what ways are the model's decisions and actions embedded in**

your process or applications?
Understand how the technology is being used and how data is integrated into your business systems. There are all kinds of possibilities but also significant ramifications waiting out there.

- ***Can I turn off AI, or is it already too ingrained in our systems?***
  I call this a Kill Switch. They're built into systems you use every day, mechanisms that turn off a system, a piece of machinery, or even a weapon. Think about what would happen if for any reason your business had to stop using an AI model. Could you do it? How?

There are many great resources for learning about how best to use AI in your enterprise. Some are listed in this book's appendix. Knowing the questions to ask will prepare you for the next wave of disruptive innovations. The most critical question that all creators, scientists, and engineers should ask themselves is *Who is accountable for the outcome?*

Keep in mind that *you* are the product.

Bjork: Consciousness Notes for The Road

With the sudden proliferation of artificial intelligence, we're seeing more reflection on what it means to be human and hearing more mentions of consciousness. This has been part of my awareness and area of study for the last couple of decades, but it was during my time in seminary that my understanding really deepened. As an Interfaith/Inter-spiritual Reverend—and a bit of a science nerd—I am delighted to have open dialogues about what makes us human and where we fit in the cosmic evolution.

Consciousness is still debated by experts who have yet to prove its true source or even agree on a definition. Consciousness can be described as sentience, an awareness of internal and external experiences. A neuroscientist might say it's part of our brain function. Doctors describe it as a state of being awake and aware. Religious leaders might attribute it to God. It can be subjective.

In examining leadership, let's look beyond these pigeonholed ideas of consciousness and feel into three different levels:

1. Consciousness as related to Self

2. Consciousness as expressed in different groups and cultures

3. Consciousness as an energetic field of evolutionary intelligence

Self: Though we use phrases like "my consciousness" or "your consciousness," consciousness itself doesn't change. Its variables are created from on our own beliefs and emotional state. Think of emotions as different points on a receiver. Feelings that drain energy—shame, grief, apathy, anger, hate, fear—live way over at the low end of the scale, blocking our access to consciousness. High-frequency emotions like courage, acceptance, reason, joy, love, and peace lead us to consciousness. A conscious leader tunes their beliefs, emotions, and actions to the energy of consciousness.

Groups: Different consciousness levels have emerged around "values" as organizing principles of human nature. A system called Spiral Dynamics, which outlines distinct levels and tiers of consciousness development, posits that groups—companies, cultures, and societies—connect by finding commonalities. Members don't agree on every issue, but they connect over shared values; the way they experience the world.

Consciousness levels dating back five or even ten thousand years still prevail today in many places. The consciousness of business hasn't changed much in the last 300 years. Many companies and leaders continue to cling to the old paradigm and systems that benefit those in power. It's not on pace with evolutionary development or the potential of this era. Effective leaders who want to create big impact will need a higher organizing principle for consciousness.

Fields: Leaders should expand their awareness to include the energetic field of evolutionary intelligence that we call Consciousness. But as we Swedes say, "A beloved child has many names." Evolutionary intelligence is sometimes referred to as Universal Intelligence, Unified Field, Collective Consciousness, or Infinite Mind. Whatever we call it and whatever pulls its strings, let's be clear about a couple of things:

As a leader in the big leagues, strive for connection with evolutionary intelligence (Consciousness), especially when decisions must be made. It's a peerless advantage for creativity, innovation, and human relationships. Everything in the Universe is connected to everything else. In a cosmic field of oneness, you can sense what's going on far beyond your local self.

Evolutionary intelligence isn't something we have. It's something we *are*. We "live it" in our own unique vessels to support human evolution.

The onslaught of artificial intelligence applications means leaders will have to find deeper answers about what it means to be human. AI feels exciting but threatening. Aside from existential trepidation, people are afraid it's coming for their jobs. They want to be assured that they are special and safe, that they could never be replaced by machines. In response to AI, we should examine the benefits of being human. It's our Unique Selling Proposition, after all.

1. Emotions set humans apart from machines. A capacity for human connection is one of the best advantages a business leader can have, because at the core, business is just interactions between human beings.

2. Our own emotions do not define us or reality. They shape our *perception* of reality. Your present-moment awareness, your ability to consciously connect and let life happen through you, is the jewel of your humanity.

3. Artificial intelligence has put the Information Age on steroids. It's important to remember that AI can reflect back only what it's been fed, so its performance is based in part on our flaws. It can be compared to the ego, the survival function that always wants more, will do anything to get it, and can never have enough. Its potentially destructive powers mean the ego has to be trained to stay in its place. We should think of AI as a great tool, but never let it be in charge. You have to be in charge. You, a beautiful expression of conscious awareness. You have to call the shots in resonance with

your evolutionary intelligence and use the tools that serve your higher vision.

As lofty as these concepts of consciousness, cosmic evolution, and different forms of intelligence may seem, they are practical and effective when applied to technological advances and leadership tactics. An understanding of what makes us human can keep us from creating our own obsolescence or causing our own demise. Humans have never even come close to using their full potential. We can be so much more.

A humbling but liberating reflection for leaders amid this transmutational storm of technology is the realization that we're not the end product. Evolution won't stop at what we now call being human. We think of ourselves as top of the food chain, kings of the world. We're not. It's been 13.8 billion years since the Universe heaved a great sigh and created the first hydrogen atom that became a large part of every human's atomic percentage. We don't know what comes next, but we can use our best intentions to set an evolutionary course that will make future species glad that we were here.

We have reached a unique point in the evolution of creation when we can experience consciousness through the lens of humanity. As Geoffrey Hinton said, "Humanity is just a passing phase for evolutionary Intelligence."

When you're making decisions, stay connected to human integrity by considering these questions:

- *Am I present while making decisions? Do I feel aligned with my values?* If you feel non-present or out of alignment, bring yourself back through presence training.

- *What is my emotional state? Do I feel peaceful, courageous, and joyful, or angry, resentful, or vindictive?* Get to a place of peace to have a more powerful impact.

- *What is my intention for this project/model? Why do I want to pursue it?* Check your ego and don't be satisfied until your answer includes big-picture goodness.

- *How do I position my teams to regularly connect to evolutionary intelligence? What type of training do humans need to do good things and deliver good results?* Find out and then pull out every stop to provide that support.

- *Which human aspects are needed to make a project or model successful?* The heart is hard to measure, as are kindness, empathy, and team flow. Develop reward systems and incentives that encourage people to be good humans.

- *Will this project/model so greatly diminish the need for human abilities that its use will cause us to atrophy?* Nature will only develop systems it deems necessary. Your responsibility is to make sure that the long-term consequences of your undertakings don't reverse human development.

We can't put the butterfly back in the cocoon. We can't unscramble eggs.

Let's human well together.

--

"Never ruin your present for a past that has no future."

~ Dalai Lama

--

Fourteen
Enter with Mind Skills

As this book concludes and you continue on your journey to the big leagues, we want to make it easy for you to always use your best mind skills. Three simple prompts:

Stop. Unleash. Lead.

That's our mantra. It won't mean anything to someone who hasn't read this book and acquired Mind Skills, but it will to you. Keep these key reminders in mind as you travel the exciting road ahead.

Stop

"Stop" is one of the most valuable prompts you can give yourself. As we've said, humans have an array of automated functions and erroneous programming that dictate our reactions and try to make decisions for us. When you sense that stir, remember that your reaction likely is based on things that are no longer true, or that don't serve you.

"Stop" also means to stop in on ourselves, to look inward and check in. You can meditate or engage in any practice that makes your mind calm and non-reactive. If mindfulness or other meditation techniques aren't for you, just close your eyes and listen to the air conditioner for fifteen minutes. That's all it takes. When you're in a state of stillness, the judging, assessing, controlling part of your mind can let go of old, limiting programs and enter a larger state of consciousness. Mind-calming practices like meditation are the brain Roomba we talked about. You brush your teeth at least a couple of times a day. Mental hygiene is as important as dental hygiene. They're daily practices that keep our systems from eroding.

The more you practice intentional stops the better you'll get at stopping when it really matters. When workplace power plays and disappointments occur, summon stillness and take stock of what's real and true. Remember who you are and what's important to you and you won't get caught up in drama. You'll use your emotional stamina on meaningful things.

Imagine there's a big, closed red door inside your mind. On the other side lies higher executive functioning, unparalleled clarity, and unlimited creativity. The only way through is to first stop within yourself and then walk right up to that door and consciously turn the knob. Otherwise, you'll flee back to your old ways and outdated tools.

Stopping sometimes brings up old fears or wounds. It takes courage to stop so often and so well that it becomes more comfortable than the old unhelpful past.

Continue to practice connecting with your stillness, heart space, and compassion for self. Find grace as you exit relationships, roles, or companies. Always own your own bullshit. Be fearless but forgiving toward both self and others.

Never forget that the most powerful you can be—alone; in a room; or on a stage—is in your own stillness and presence. The most powerful mind is a peaceful mind. Be sure to stop in often.

Unleash

Use your new mind skills to unleash the best of yourself. Keep developing them and revisit them often. Don't squander your potential. Now is the time to show the world the best of you—the whole, authentic, unique you.

You can't unleash the best of what other people think you should be. It must be yours.

As you learn to unleash the best of you, your friendships and communities will shift a little. You'll see who your real friends are. When you become impactful and popular, some may not seem very happy for you, while others will show up all set to play. It's all good. Everyone's on their own journey and they may not yet have had the call to self-actualize. Keep operating from heart-based conscious awareness and be the most peaceful, powerful you. Stop before you unleash.

Imagine again the big red door. You open it and see abilities you didn't know you had, opportunities you've never dared to dream. You see relationships that will bring new levels of meaning, impact, and joy.

As you stand in the doorway, a chorus of voices within will tell you to shut the door. *Who are you to be so fabulous?* Who are you *not* to be? You are a life-giving seed in soil, not a dead rock in dirt.

You can walk through the door by practicing one of the easiest mind skills: Gratitude. The energy of gratitude will let you connect to everything beyond that door. The modern world has ways to distract you from your bigger mission and deeper joy. Keep using and fine-tuning your bullshit radar. Pay attention to what's going on above the ambient noise. Keep putting yourself in situations that allow for growth and inner expansion. That's how you unleash your potential and become ready to lead at higher levels.

Lead

You came here to gain mind skills. You kept your focus and stayed with it all the way through. That tells us you are one of the leaders the world awaits:

The kind who leads with constant self-awareness and conscious awareness of people and the world.

Great leaders love to learn.

A willingness to learn will take you far. Make the decision to stay curious about things that interest you, that you feel passionate about. Be curious about the people you meet. How fascinating that their opinions can be the opposite of yours! How interesting that words don't always mean the same thing to them that they do to you! How wonderful that someone from a totally different background is enriching you with their perspective.

Being excited is a decision too. Choose to be excited about the projects in front of you. Be intentional about what you want to have happen in the world. Feel excitement for seeing work come to fruition. Find enthusiasm in even the small, seemingly insignificant or unrelated things. It will make you a better leader because excitement, like other high-frequency emotions, is contagious.

Great leaders learn to love.

You can't lead your teams if you don't love your teams. You won't succeed with your projects if you don't love your projects. Just like curiosity and excitement, love is a choice. You can choose to focus on what's annoying and wrong, or on what's good and helpful.

When you walk through the big red door you are entering sacred ground. Stay in the world of evolved leadership and carry your consciousness and self-awareness everywhere with you. Be clear in your intention and your attention. Know that your primary job as a leader is to create more great leaders.

And now you know how.

--

"I always had a repulsive need to be something more than human. I felt very puny as a human. I thought, 'F*k that. I want to be a superhuman.'"

- David Bowie

--

Acknowledgments

We both want to extend our heartfelt gratitude to everyone who has inspired us to create this book, including all the readers who are taking courageous steps on their leadership journeys. A special thank you to our talented editor Jodie Remick.

Linda's Acknowledgments:

What a ride! I want to express my reverence and deepest appreciation to my mentors and wisdom teachers Dr. Robert Holden, Rev. Diane Berke, and Dr. Kurt Johnson.

Thank you to my many brothers and sisters in the Evolutionary Leaders circle and Unity Earth, especially Adam C. Hall, Dr. Jude Currivan, Rev. Deborah Moldow, Ben Bowler, Jon and Sommer Ramer, and Sister Jenna, with special thanks to Chief Dwaine Perry of the Ramapo Munsee Lunaape Indian Nation.

My deep gratitude extends to all those who have inspired and supported me over the years in the development and fine-tuning of Mindfulness Intelligence®, including my business brother Mark A. Pfister.

To the students, participants, and audiences who have courageously opened their minds and hearts in their leadership transformation, thank you. You have taught me as well, more than you know.

A big thank-you to the bosses who shaped me early in my career, especially Chuck Winner and Lance Brisson who believed in me and granted me such generous space for growth. Chuck, I hope you are running free with the wild horses.

A special "Tack" to Renée Lundholm, Gunilla Girardo, Kristiina Helenius, Ulrika "Red" Nilsson, and Yasmine Månsson for bridging the gap between Scandinavia and the United States.

Deepest thanks to my co-author Stephanie, that rare type of leader who balances the powerful forward motion of business with the wisdom of the self-reflective pause. An extra gold star is awarded for her gutsiness in bringing Mindfulness Intelligence to her leadership teams long before the "soft stuff" was accepted. She is a model of courage and leadership vision.

Last but not least, I want to thank my dad, Claes Bjork, for having engaged me in valuable conversations about leadership all my life.

In loving memory of Björn Karlsson.

Stephanie's Acknowledgments:

Writing this book has been a deeply personal and reflective journey. It's been a privilege to share my own experiences and insights from my path to the C-Suite.

I'm grateful for the support, guidance, and inspiration I received from those who played a significant role in shaping my professional journey. I thank the present and former executive teams at Charter, Cadent, and Cablevision for having supported me throughout my journey. I am indebted to these organizations' many visionary leaders, who empowered me to take risks, embrace challenges, and step outside my comfort zone. There are too many to list here, but special thanks to Tom Rutledge, John Bickham, Jim Blackley, Barry Baker, and the late Wilt Hildebrand.

To my own team members, both past and present, I thank you for your hard work, dedication, and commitment. Your contributions, creativity, and shared vision have been pivotal in realizing our collective goals. I am honored to have worked alongside you. Thank you, Margaret VanGulden, Marti Moore, Louis Fischetti and Joe Godas, for coming along with me and always being there.

None of this would have been possible without my amazing support team: Valerie Raffo, Barbara LaVardera, and Julie Pontier. You have put up with me and kept me on track for the past 20+ years. I am honored to call you friends.

To all those who have played a part, big or small, in my journey, thank you.

To Linda, my co-author, confidant, colleague, and friend, thank you for teaming up for this journey. This book was born from our collaboration. It's been a joy creating with you.

To my husband David Beale, and all my friends and family, no words could express the grateful appreciation I carry in my heart. A special call-out to my dad, Leonard Steffek, for encouraging me to pursue a career in engineering and for the great conversations about projects that if we told anyone about, we'd have to kill them.

Finally, I want to express my gratitude to the readers of this book. I hope that Linda's and my journey will be a source of inspiration, encouragement, and guidance to those who aspire to reach the C-Suite or pursue their goals, both personal or professional, with voracious curiosity.

Reading & Resources

Book recommendations and other resources for further exploration.

Chapter 1 - Exit With Grace

Wherever You Go, There You Are, by Jon Kabat Zinn

Give and Take – Why Helping Others Drives Our Success, by Adam Grant

The Biology of Belief, by Dr Bruce Lipton

Chapter 2 - Owning Your Shit

How to Do the Work: Recognize Your Patterns, Heal from Your Past, and Create Your Self, by Dr. Nicole LePera

Radical Forgiveness – A Revolutionary Five-Stage Process to Heal Relationships, Let Go of Anger and Blame, and Find Peace in Any Situation, by Colin Tipping

Chapter 3 - Be The Cleaning Lady

Super Brain – Unleashing the Explosive Power of Your Mind to Maximize Health, Happiness, and Spiritual Well-being, by Deepak Chopra, M.D. and Rudolph E. Tanzi, Ph.D.

Altered Traits – Science Reveals How Meditation Changes Your Mind, Brain, and Body, by Daniel Goleman and Richard J. Davidson

The Polyvagal Theory: Neurophysiological Foundations of Emotions, Attachment, Communication, and Self-regulation, by Stephen W. Porges

Chapter 4 – Executive Confidence

Becoming Supernatural: How Common People Are Doing the Uncommon, by Dr. Joe Dispenza

Atomic Habits: An Easy & Proven Way to Build Good Habits & Break Bad Ones, by James Clear

Chapter 5 - Big Hearted Boundaries

The Wisdom Codes: Ancient Words to Rewire Our Brains and Heal Our Hearts, by Gregg Braden

If It Hurts, It Isn't Love and 365 Other Principles to Heal and Transform Your Relationships, by Chuck Spezzano, PhD

Chapter 6 - Planted, not Buried

The Power of Now, by Eckart Tolle

Welcoming the Unwelcome, by Pema Chödrön

Chapter 7 - Grateful AND Compensated

Words of Gratitude for Mind, Body, and Soul, by Robert Emmons and Joanna Hill

The Psychology of Gratitude, by Robert Emmons and Michael McCullough

Thanks! How the New Science of Gratitude Can Make You Happier, by Robert Emmons

A Simple Act of Gratitude: How Learning to Say Thank You Changed My Life, by John Kralik

Gratitude, by Oliver Sacks

Chapter 8 - Room Reader with a Bullshit Radar

Electric Body, Electric Health, by Eileen Day McKusick

Follow Your Joy, by Dr. Robert Holden

The Body Keeps the Score; brain, mind, and body in the healing of trauma, by Bessel van der Kolk, M.D.

Chapter 9 - Future Orchestrator

Science and the Indian Tradition: When Einstein Met Tagore (India in the Modern World), by David L. Gosling

You Are the Universe: Discovering Your Cosmic Self and Why It Matters, by Deepak Chopra MD and Menas C. Kafatos PhD

The Story of Gaia: The Big Breath and the Evolutionary Journey of Our Con-

scious Planet, by Jude Currivan PhD

The Holomovement: Embracing Our Collective Purpose to Unite Humanity, by Emanuel Kuntzelman, Jill Robinson, et al.

(Rumi poem translated from Persian by Coleman Barks and John Moyne)

Chapter 10 - Helping the Team Win

BIFF At Work, Your Guide to Difficult Workplace Communication, by Bill Eddy and Megan Hunter

Think Again, by Adam Grant

Super Bosses, by Sydney Finkelstein

The Coming Interspiritual Age, by David Robert Ord and Kurt Johnson

Chapter 11 - Power Sharer

Power vs Force, by David R. Hawkins

Dare to Lead, by Brené Brown

Chapter 12 & 13 – Unscrambled Eggs & Notes for The Road

Editing Humanity: The CRISPR Revolution and the New Era of Genome Editing, by Kevin Davies

Race after Technology, by Ruha Benjamin

Max Tegmark is a physicist and AI researcher at MIT, co-founder of the Future of Life Institute, and author of Life 3.0: Being Human in the Age of Artificial Intelligence

Research:

"Toxic Workplace Culture 10 Times More Likely to Drive Employees Away", Forbes https://www.forbes.com/sites/bryanrobinson/2022/02/03/toxic-workplace-culture-10-times-more-likely-to-drive-employees-away-study-shows/

"Tough at the Top" Sarah Bond and Gillian Shapiro https://hbr.org/2015/01/what-resilience-means-and-why-it-matters

The Failure Tolerant Leader, by Richard Farson and Ralph Keyes https://hbr.org/2002/08/the-failure-tolerant-leader

VeneKlasen, L., & Miller, V. (2007). A new weave of power, people & politics: The action guide for advocacy and citizen participation. https://justassociates.org/en/resources/new-weave-power-people-politics-action-guide-advocacy-and-citizen-participation

Mathie, A., Cameron, J., & Gibson, K. (2017). Asset-based and citizen-led development: Using a diffracted power lens to analyze the possibilities and challenges. Progress in Development Studies, 17(1), 1-13. doi: 10.1177/1464993416674302 Available from http://journals.sagepub.com/doi/abs/10.1177/1464993416674302

Hunjan, R., & Keophilavon, S. (2010). Power and making change happen. Fife: Carnegie UK Trust. Available from https://www.carnegieuktrust.org.uk/publications/power-and-making-change-happen/

About the Authors

Linda Bjork

Linda Bjork heads the Inner Business Institute, is the Founder of Mindfulness Intelligence® and the Author of the leadership book "Inner Business - Training Your Mind for Leadership Success." She leads professionals all over the globe to their highest leadership potential.

Linda led a creative agency to global recognition 2004-2014, based in NYC and Stockholm, Sweden. With continued outstanding financial results and an outspoken focus on mind training for the staff, Linda became known as "the Meditating CEO." The agency won numerous awards under Linda's leadership, among them Agency of The Year 2009.

In addition to her engineering, design and business background, Linda is a Certified MBSR Leader, a Certified Success Coach, an elected Evolutionary Leader, and an Ordained Interfaith/Inter-spiritual Minister.

Stephanie Mitchko

Stephanie Mitchko-Beale is an Emmy® Award winning C-Suite executive who thrives in the space between technology and business results. She is the recent EVP & CTO at Charter Communications. As a key spokesperson and sought-after presenter, Stephanie is dedicated to raising the consciousness of leaders for a more sustainable, equitable and prosperous future. A trailblazing technology executive who has achieved remarkable success in her field. With multiple Emmy awards and a groundbreaking tech patent to her name, she embodies the epitome of leadership in the tech industry.

Prior to Joining Charter Stephanie was CTO & COO of Cadent TV. Before joining Cadent Stephanie was the SVP of Video Infrastructure Software at Cablevision, responsible for the development of the innovative Multi-Room (cloud-based) DVR system and Video On Demand.

With more than 25 years of experience, Mitchko is a technology, media, and advanced advertising maven with a solid record of pioneering evolutionary products.

Stay Connected

Stay updated for book events and speaking engagements at the Mind Skills website. Be sure to register for your free leadership gift!

www.mindskillsthebook.com

To book Linda and Stephanie for Mind Skills speaking engagements, please email info@mindskillsthebook.com.

Continue the dialogue on LinkedIn and our respective professional sites:

Find Linda Bjork
https://www.linkedin.com/in/linda-bjork-05643428/
https://www.lindabjork.org

Find Stephanie Mitchko
https://www.linkedin.com/in/stephanie-mitchko-beale-0047124/
https://www.rareairleadership.com

Printed in the USA
CPSIA information can be obtained
at www.ICGtesting.com
LVHW041955211223
767102LV00004B/520